WHAT'S NEXT

**Twenty-Two United Methodist Leaders
Discuss the Future of the Church**

CONTRIBUTORS

Tori C. Butler	Kim Goddard	Rebekah Miles
Wil Cantrell	Stephen Handy	Sue Nilson Kibbey
Kenneth L. Carder	Kristin Joyner	Randall Partin
Walter Cross	Kay Kotan	Rebekah Simon-Peter
Melanie L. Dobson	William B. Lawrence	Rodney Smothers
Christopher Donald	Richard Looney	Ryan Spurrier
Thomas E. Frank	M. Douglas Meeks	Laceye Warner

KEVIN SLIMP

Market
Square
BOOKS

WHAT'S NEXT?

Twenty-Two United Methodist Leaders
Discuss the Future of the Church

by Kevin Slimp

©2022 Market Square Publishing, LLC

books@marketsquarebooks.com
141 N. Martinwood Dr., Knoxville TN 37923

ISBN: 978-1-950899-57-9

Printed and Bound in the United States of America
Cover Illustration & Book Design ©2021 Market Square Publishing, LLC

Editors: Jean Henderson & Sheri Carder Hood
Post-Process Editor: Ken Rochelle

Scripture quotations used with permission from:

CEB

Scripture quotations from the COMMON ENGLISH BIBLE. © Copyright 2011 COMMON ENGLISH BIBLE. All rights reserved. Used by permission. (www.CommonEnglishBible.com).

ESV

The Holy Bible: English Standard Version
Scripture quotations marked "ESV" are taken from The Holy Bible: English Standard Version, copyright © 2001, Wheaton: Good News Publishers. Used by permission. All rights reserved.

MSG

Scripture quotations marked MSG are taken from THE MESSAGE, copyright © 1993, 2002, 2018 by Eugene H. Peterson. Used by permission of NavPress, represented by Tyndale House Publishers. All rights reserved.

NASB

Scripture quotations taken from the (NASB®) New American Standard Bible®, Copyright © 1960, 1971, 1977, 1995, 2020 by The Lockman Foundation. Used by permission. All rights reserved. www.lockman.org

NRSV

New Revised Standard Version Bible, copyright © 1989 National Council of the Churches of Christ in the United States of America. Used by permission. All rights reserved worldwide.

NIV

Scriptures marked NIV are taken from the NEW INTERNATIONAL VERSION (NIV): Scripture taken from THE HOLY BIBLE, NEW INTERNATIONAL VERSION ®. Copyright© 1973, 1978, 1984, 2011 by Biblica, Inc.™. Used by permission of Zondervan

J.B. Phillips

Scripture quotations marked "Phillips" are taken from The New Testament in Modern English, copyright © 1958, 1959, 1960 J.B. Phillips and 1947, 1952, 1955, 1957 The Macmillian Company, New York. Used by permission. All rights reserved.

Table of Contents

INTRODUCTION
So, What's Next?

Kevin Slimp

Like many of you, I've had several careers. I spent my twenties and early thirties working in United Methodist congregations as a youth leader. Thanks to one of my mentors, Leo Rippy, Jr. – who was serving a temporary gig leading the Board of Discipleship – I learned many of the ins and outs of denominational bureaucracy at an early age. While I served as president of the United Methodist Youth Workers Association in the late 1980s, Leo invited me to work with the Board of Discipleship many times. I often traveled to Nashville to represent youth leaders on various projects.

I drew the attention of denominational leaders from time to time and found myself meeting with bishops and other church leaders to oversee research, submit legislation to General Conference (bishops couldn't do that, but I could), and once, I even assisted a retiring bishop as he and his wife moved to another state. I remember those times fondly.

Thanks to some work I did in the mid-1990s that led to the development of a popular technology, I found myself in the role of "recognized expert" in areas outside the church. There were years I would speak at conferences in more than a hundred cities, and an increasing number of folks seemed to be interested in what I had to say about various topics. I spoke at publishers' conventions, government conferences, and gatherings of economists, photographers, and journalists.

I've been a guest lecturer at more than a hundred colleges and universities and the warmup act at more political debates (while speaking for journalism groups) than I can remember. I was often called on to talk to groups of faculty members about my vision of the future. "On the side," I directed a program at the University of Tennessee. I've spoken to audiences at the National Press Club in Washington, D.C., and legislative events in several states and countries. I've written syndicated columns for magazines and newspapers read weekly and monthly by millions of readers. Well-known business leaders from North America, Europe, and Asia would call me for advice or assistance. In that world, I was the expert.

Sometime in the middle of all that, I served four years as director of communications for a United Methodist conference. Five years ago, possibly to hold AARP at bay as long as possible, I started a publishing company (Market Square Books). It's not my first, but it is my first in the church world.

Wait...I take that back. I almost forgot about Insight Publishing, a company my friend Ron Schmidt – now a retired minister from California – and I began in our late twenties to create program materials for youth groups. At one point, more than two-thousand churches of all types were subscribing to our materials. I doubt I will ever forget the day Jerry Falwell – yes, Jerry Falwell, Sr. – called our office to find out "who our church is buying program materials from."

Dr. Falwell asked a simple-yet-tricky question: "What does your company believe?"

Thankfully, Ron answered the phone that day and was quick on his feet. After a brief pause, Ron answered, "We believe in God, the Father Almighty, creator of heaven and earth; And in Jesus Christ, his only Son our Lord; who was conceived by the Holy Spirit, born of the Virgin Mary, suffered under Pontius Pilate, was crucified, dead, and buried. The third day he rose from the dead; he ascended into heaven, and is seated at the right hand of the Father, and will come again to judge the living and the dead."

There was silence for just a moment as we waited for a response from Dr. Falwell. Then came his words, "Well, I guess I can't argue with that."

Now I publish books – approximately seventy of them over the past five years. I'm quite comfortable knowing that I'm not the expert anymore, at least not in this world. Today I work with the experts. I spend time daily with brilliant thinkers representing various areas of leadership in the church. So, it was natural for me to sit at my computer, write thirty or so United Methodist leaders – clergy and laypersons – and ask each to write a chapter answering the simple-yet-tricky question, "What's Next?" Twenty-one of them answered "yes," and I added my name to even out the list at twenty-two writers.

Some readers will remember a book we at Market Square Publishing published in 2019 titled, *Where Do We Go from Here?* It topped Amazon's best-seller list in the Methodist genre for three months. With the significant assistance of Bishop Kenneth Carder, I gathered twenty-four United Methodist leaders of various theological viewpoints together to answer the question, "Where do we go from here?"

This time around, I took a different approach as I wrote each prospective writer. In that first email, I wrote, "My guess is most of us will still be United Methodists after the next General Conference, and we should give serious thought to the future of our branch of Christianity. Would you join me in sharing your response to the question, 'What's next?'"

Their assignment was open-ended. As you'll soon find, some answered the question from the individual viewpoint, tackling topics like personal prayer and Bible study. Others responded by writing about the local church and how churches might approach the future. Others answered from a denominational standpoint.

I purposely placed chapters by Bishop Richard Looney and Rev. Walter Cross at the beginning and end of the book. Both chapters inspire hope. Not sugar-coated hope like you might find on a Facebook post but authentic, inspired hope.

Frankly, there is no grand scheme in the arrangement of the other chapters. As the manuscripts arrived from the writers, the files went straight to the editors, Jean Henderson and Sheri Carder Hood; they went back to the authors for one last look-through and then onto the pages.

I am eternally grateful to each of these writers. They will not be receiving royalty payments. They answered the call to write because they care about our church. Royalties, as with the 2019 book, are being donated to UMCOR.

What's next? Don't ask me. I'm not the expert. Fortunately, the experts share their thoughts on the pages that follow.

Kevin Slimp makes his home in Knoxville, Tennessee. He says his "day job" is publisher at Market Square Books. Kevin founded and directed The University of Tennessee Newspaper Institute from 1997-2017. He is the author of several books, including *The Good Folks of Lennox Valley, Who Killed A.J. Fryerson?,* and *Where Do We Go From Here?* From 2015-2020, his syndicated column titled "The Good Folks of Lennox Valley" appeared weekly in more than 300 newspapers and magazines. Currently, his columns related to journalism are carried in professional publications in North America, Europe, Asia and Australia. Kevin is the founder of ClergyEducation.com and Kevin Slimp's Online Academy and, in his spare time, continues to be a popular convention speaker among communications professionals.

CHAPTER ONE
Do No Harm, Do Good

Bishop Richard Looney

But to you who are listening I say: Love your enemies, do good to those who hate you, bless those who curse you, pray for those who mistreat you. If someone slaps you on one cheek, turn to them the other also. If someone takes your coat, do not withhold your shirt from them. Give to everyone who asks you, and if anyone takes what belongs to you, do not demand it back. Do to others as you would have them do to you.

Luke 6:27-31 (NIV)

These are complex and uncertain times. So many things that we relied upon are unsettled. There seems to be a storm of mistrust brewing in the nation and the church. Hope for the end of the pandemic evaporated as we fought over masks and vaccinations. Even after a record-breaking turnout in our federal election, many of us continue to cry fraud. In our own denomination, we looked forward to a General Conference that would either show us a way to our future or give us a way to separate without doing further harm.

Uncertainty about the continuing mutations of the virus, the future of American democracy, and the shape of our church leave us almost in despair. As anxiety threatens to overwhelm us, we run the risk of becoming mentally, emotionally, and spiritually ill. If that occurs, we risk becoming part of the deepening division, not a part of the solution.

While none of us would propose that we have the ultimate solution, allow me to suggest some modest proposals that can influence the way we treat each other going forward. We want our discussions and

5

decisions to bring healing, not further harm. Should the proposed separation be adopted, we would pray it would be constructive and not destructive. We would hope that we would honor our kinship as a part of the Wesleyan family and exhibit the Spirit of Christ in our treatment of one another.

John Wesley expected all who continued in the Societies to "do no harm; do good and attend upon the ordinances of God." He listed as harmful:

- Quarreling

- Brawling

- Railing

Especially harmful was doing to others as you would not have them do to you. Doing good was being in every way kind and merciful to all.

From these general principles come a few suggestions:

Respect the worth of those with whom we disagree.

It is too easy to demonize our so-called opponents. They are not only wrong but somehow less worthy. It might seem appealing to belong to a group that agrees on all the significant issues. That, however, could be more deadly than imagined. My own faith has been challenged and stretched by serving churches made up of moderates, liberals, conservatives; independents, democrats, republicans; high, low, and blended worshippers. The tension is not always comfortable, but our common loyalty to Christ has enabled us to grow as we learn from each other. As I call to remembrance many of their faces, I can't imagine the church saying, "We have no need of you."

Early in my ministry, I shared a concern with my dad, also a pastor. One of my churches wanted to invite a preacher they knew to preach their annual revival. I thought his theology was very unacceptable. Dad said I should go ahead and invite him. "He is a much better man than his theology."

So reluctantly, I issued the invitation. Sure enough, he was a remarkable man who became a dear friend. He loved God and people and was a compelling preacher. His generosity was an inspiration to all.

When we get to know people better, we discover that they are a strange mixture of the good and bad. And when we get to know ourselves, we find out that we too have our blind spots, unrecognized prejudices, and weaknesses.

Much of the heat in our discussions come not from our disagreements but from our becoming disagreeable. Most of us merely want to be respected, not necessarily agreed with. In Luke 6:27, Jesus gives instructions about loving our enemies, doing good to our haters, and praying for those who abuse us. Should we be expected to do any less for our brothers and sisters in the United Methodist Church? Then Jesus adds that we should do to others as we would have them do to us. The measure one gives in judging will be the measure we get back.

We need to recognize our own limitations.

We are a strange mixture of good and bad with blind spots, prejudices, and weaknesses. I had a brilliant friend who would say, "I am often wrong, but never in doubt." Often, that is true for us.

Leslie Weatherhead, the famed English preacher, described having a drawer labeled "Awaiting further light." There he would place complex questions that required humility and further study.

Most of us would agree that our recent debates have been ugly, destructive, and harmful, even embarrassing. We have sounded harsh and self-righteous rather than sharing our heartfelt convictions with humility and love.

One of the most graphic images used by Jesus was the man with a log in his eye busily attempting to remove the speck from a neighbor's eye in Matthew 7:4.

Nor has the Church always had a clear vision of essential truth. We used our interpretation of the Scriptures to justify slavery, the torture of enemies, the silencing of women, the separation of races, the dominance of men. When I was a teenager, I realized that my father was working with a couple who were "living together in open sin." He was encouraging them to seal their relationship in marriage. After a year, they agreed to do so and asked him to perform the ceremony. Our *Discipline* forbade performing a ceremony for anyone who had been divorced. When he explained the situation and offered to find another pastor, the woman said," That's the strangest thing I ever heard."

In subsequent years that prohibition was removed by the General Conference. The conference continues to meet every four years (until the pandemic) to refine and upgrade the *Discipline*. For more than 50 years, we have struggled to find a way forward together on the matter of same-sex unions. That agreement has eluded us and brought us to this moment of crisis. As we continue the struggle, we need to combine respect for our brothers and sisters with a measure of genuine personal humility.

We can see people as individuals loved by God, not some non-descript category.

The son or daughter of my friends, or a member of my class or church, sounds different from liberal or conservative; Republican or Democrat; believer or non-believer; native or immigrant; young or old. Each of us has experienced the sting of being placed in a category that completely misses the richness of who we are. I am often shamed by the misjudgments I make in early impressions. The conservative displays surprising touches of liberal action; the liberal flashes of tradition; the old act youthful, the young stuck in traditions.

While serving in the South Georgia area, I saw a clear example of our tendency to ignore an individual's uniqueness because of their category. One of the district superintendents asked a committee about their openness to a woman pastor. The answer was typical, "We should be, but we are not ready yet."

A committee member asked a man who was the strongest objector a question: "You wouldn't want Joyce P. as your preacher?" Joyce had preached there recently and was warmly received, having a radiant faith and unusual skill as a speaker. He answered, "I would love to have Joyce. I just don't want a woman."

We realized that we needed to talk about Joyce or Mary, not an unnamed woman. How often I continue to miss the opportunity to appreciate the worth of someone because I see them as old or young, male or female, conservative or liberal, gay or straight. When I remember that an individual is the son or daughter of someone I love or the child of the Lord I serve, my attitude tends to change dramatically. Even my disapproval of their actions takes on a different flavor.

We can remind ourselves that the church is to embody the Spirit of Christ.

One of my favorite descriptions for the church is simply but profoundly as the Body of Christ. We tend to label our local church as orthodox or progressive, traditional or contemporary, formal or informal. And we each have our own preference. But more basic is our reflection of the love of Christ and our love of our neighbor.

Of course, we all fall short. The church is made up of imperfect instruments. And the wonder is that God uses such people, including you and me. God's love for the world and those who inhabit it is so great that imperfect instruments are used to serve and bless. It's a wonder that God can use me in ministry. It's also a wonder that God uses people that I may not think are adequate or proper. And we may help people more when we confess or share our struggles than when we tout our victories.

 A tragic outcome of any future separation would be the creation of two self-righteous denominations. Ray Stevens' classic *Mississippi Squirrel Revival* song had the phrase, "The First Self-Righteous Church of Pascagoula, Mississippi." In Luke 18:9, Jesus told the parable of those who trusted in themselves that they were righteous and regarded others with contempt. "Those who exalt themselves will be humbled."

In 1983 Carolyn and I did a pulpit exchange in Australia. One of the gifts we cherished was an Australian hymnal. I have recently begun using it as a supplement in my devotional reading. A hymn of John White Chadwick (1840-1904) has become my prayer for the United Methodist Church:

We are of thee, the children of thy love; the brothers of Thy well-beloved Son; descend, O Holy Spirit, into our hearts, that we may be as one; as one with Thee, to whom we ever trend; as one with him, our Brother and our Friend. We would be one with the joy that breaks into song; one with the grief that trembles into prayer; One with the power that makes the children free to follow truth, and thus to follow Thee.

Finally, above all, may we renew our faith in the wonder of God's wisdom, power, and love. Out of nothing, when God spoke, Creation blossomed. Out of the chaos of the present moment, may God bring light and direction. As divided and uncertain as we appear, may we still be used as instruments of reconciliation.

Our task is even now to make disciples for the transformation of the world. John Greenleaf Whittier's classic hymn can become our prayer:

Within the maddening maze of things,
When tossed by storm and flood,
To one fixed trust my spirit clings;
I know that God is good!

I know not where His islands lift
Their fronded palms in air;
I only know I cannot drift
Beyond His love and care.[1]

Richard Carl Looney was born in the Methodist parsonage at Hillsville, Virginia. He graduated from Emory and Henry College and Candler School of Theology, with additional study in the University of Edinburgh, Scotland and Union Theological Seminary, Richmond, Virginia.

The Southeastern Jurisdictional Conference elected Richard Carl Looney to the episcopacy in 1988. He was assigned to the newly-created South Georgia Area, where he served until his retirement in 2000.

---

1 John Greenleaf Whittier, *Within the Maddening Maze,* 1851.

CHAPTER TWO
Called to Covenant

Laceye Warner

At the heart of Wesley's covenant prayer is vocation – hearing and following God's call upon our lives. Vocation derives from the Latin word for calling – *vocare*, though neither of these words has a clear meaning in our time and context. Their use varies across traditions. Yet, for Wesley and Methodists today, the covenant prayer frames faithful responses to God's call. The Covenant Prayer featured as the climactic moment in the annual Covenant Service in which early Methodists participate each New Year. It carries a long tradition of communal covenant between individuals, congregations, and God. While this chapter may or may not be read at the beginning of a New Year, as United Methodists we are experiencing a climactic moment in our shared journey.

Frederick Buechner described God's calling upon an individual as "the kind of work (a) that you need most to do, and (b) that the world most needs to have done...The place God calls you to is the place where your deep gladness and the world's deep hunger meet."[1] This is all very inspiring – but does not reveal the grittiness of maintaining our covenant with God in faithfulness to God's call upon our lives.

In Scripture, vocation most often refers to (1) a calling to faith in God – a calling we all share by our baptisms through the grace of the triune God – and (2) a calling to a special task on behalf of God.[2] According to Scripture, there are layers to our vocation – some shared, some individual, but always in the context of the body of Christ, and always

---

[1] Frederick Buechner, *Wishful Thinking: Revised Edition*, HarperOne, 1993.

[2] William Placher, *Callings: Twenty Centuries of Christian Wisdom on Vocation*, Eerdmans, 2005.

unfolding. As in Scripture, when we pray Wesley's Covenant Prayer, we are declaring our faith, but also our willingness to receive this unfolding, to be sent in ministry for some special task on behalf of God.

This is not always easy. Indeed, if we survey even a small number of scripture narratives, we find that God can send anyone, to go anywhere, at any time, to do anything ... despite the risks, difficulty or obstacles.

For example: Abraham and Sarah (Genesis 12.1-5a; 17.1-5; 15-17; 18.9-15); Eli and Samuel (I Samuel 3.1-10); Saul (I Samuel 9. 1-6; 18-21); Esther (4.5-17); the Disciples (Matthew 4.18-22); the Marys (Mark 16.1-8, 9-11); and Paul (Acts 9.1-20). Each story demonstrates an affirmation, or re-affirmation, of calling to faith as well as a calling to a special task on behalf of God. None of the stories is without tension and struggle.

Somehow I want to expect that living out our Christian faith is easy, straightforward, safe, and without pain or disappointment. That in praying the Wesleyan Covenant Prayer, my obedience to God's call is sealed almost effortless...no complexity or resistance. But that is not what we find in Scripture. Hearing and following God's call upon our lives can be frustrating, exhausting, even life-threatening.

The story of Jonah is an excellent example. Often Jonah is misunderstood – he is sometimes accused of being unfaithful, particularly to God's call. It is true, Jonah was reluctant to travel to Nineveh and deliver God's message of doom fleeing instead to Tarshish. But it was not due to a lack of faith or even a lack of compassion – after all, Jonah sacrificed himself by jumping overboard in the midst of a storm, to save his sailing mates from danger.

If we may participate in some creative interpretation – Jonah is a pertinent case study related to the Wesleyan Covenant Prayer – an inside perspective, if you will. We might extrapolate that Jonah would have taken very seriously the invitation to enter into Covenant with God in this manner and subsequently declined, catching a boat for some other exotic location – far from Bristol, England (a key location in the rise of early Methodism).

To be fair, Jonah did fulfill his "covenant," though ever so reluctantly. After his expulsion from the abdominal cavity of a large fish, Jonah traveled to Nineveh delivering God's message of doom. It is only in chapter Jonah Chapter 4 that the narrator reveals what some interpret as a sincere and earnest statement on Jonah's part.

O Lord! Is this not what I said while I was still in my own country? That is why I fled to Tarshish at the beginning; for I knew that you are a gracious God and merciful, slow to anger, and abounding in steadfast love, and ready to relent from punishing.

Jonah 4:2 (NRSV)

Jonah lacked obedience initially, but for the most part fulfilled God's calling to a specific task – while demonstrating deep faith and knowledge of God's steadfast love and mercy, if alongside anger and resentment.

> *Wesley urged that authentic spiritual formation could not take place, "without society, without living and conversing with others."*

In chapter 4:1 the text says God's change of mind was displeasing to Jonah – Jonah is angry. He is angry that once he delivers God's message of judgment, knowing God as he does, God will then relent, prove gracious and therefore place Jonah in a difficult spot by making him appear to be a false prophet undermining Jonah's social position.

In our reading, Jonah does not lack belief in God. He has faith in God and understands the responsibilities arising from that faith. Instead he is reluctant to obey a particular divine command, seeing in advance (accurately!) the difficulties to which such obedience will subject him. That said, he is willing bravely to throw himself overboard (1.12) when his fellow sailors fear for their lives in the midst of a torrential storm. After casting himself overboard, ironically the sailors are converted by this rogue prophet – revealing Jonah's selectivity of service.

Jonah is willing to show compassion and risk his very life for the sailors, Gentiles, but not willing to extend God's message of admonition to the Ninevites – knowing the possibility of God's gracious response to their repentance.

As we prepare to pray the Wesleyan Covenant Prayer – like, Jonah, where is our Nineveh? Is it a selectivity or exception to our willingness to serve God?

Or, with Abram and Sarah, perhaps we find God's call to a special task unbelievable? Like Eli, are we being invited to teach another how to hear and respond to God's call at our own expense? With Saul, do we find ourselves chasing donkeys? Or risking our life for our people with Esther? Perhaps we are confronted with a command like the disciples to drop our nets and follow Jesus? With Mary, fleeing in fear, yet proclaiming the gospel in the face of unbelief? Or with Paul leaving behind our status, prestige, and power to be imprisoned, among other things, for Jesus.

Unlike Jonah we can find joy in God's calling upon our lives, even in the midst of the difficulty, if we allow ourselves to remain close to God through means of grace, such as practices of piety and mercy. John Wesley claimed in his sermon "Causes of the Inefficacies of Christianity" that there were so few real Christians formed by the church of his day because Christian communities often lacked (1) a sufficient understanding of doctrine, (2) adequate discipline, (3) and self-denial.

These practices guard against Mary McLeod Bethune's admonition:

The church is beginning to acquire new courage in the application to life of the great moral truths...But too often these principles are merely preached in beautiful language when there is a pressing need to set them forth in the specific language of deed.[3]

Wesley's emphasis upon discipline, or Christian practices through the means of grace, follows Aristotle's guidance for cultivating virtue. In his Nichomachean Ethics, Aristotle explains: one becomes just by doing just acts, temperate by doing temperate acts, brave by doing brave acts. Christian practices, or the means of grace, are not meant as simple routine or obligation, but offer a means of freedom from which to hear and follow God's call to be formed in faith.

Wesley urged that authentic spiritual formation could not take place, "without society, without living and conversing with others." Jonah seemingly attempted to discern his response to God's call alone. We are not alone – we are baptized into the body of Christ, surrounded by

---

[3] Mary McLeod Bethune, "Girding for Peace," Mary McLeod Bethune Foundation Papers, Daytona Beach, Florida, n.d., 6, quoted in Clarence G. Newsome, "Mary McLeod Bethune and the Methodist Episcopal Church North: In but Out," in *This Far By Faith: Readings in African-American Women's Religious Biography*, eds. Judith Weisenfeld and Richard Newman, Routledge, 1996.

the communion of saints and embraced by the love of the Triune God. We, particularly here, are so privileged with a rich community of faith immersed in the joy of our salvation.

The Covenant Prayer is not to be taken lightly. This is serious Christianity. It is the substance of our calling to faith in the Triune God, and in readiness to be sent in ministry of any kind on behalf of God. Most importantly, we do not embark on this journey alone but in the gracious and everlasting arms of a good God who sent Jesus, God's only son, on a special task to redeem all creation through his life, death, and resurrection.

With faithfulness to God's call, difficulty and struggle may come, even grief. With faithfulness to God's call also comes joy – the joy of receiving God's salvation and participating in the unfolding reign of God.

God's burden is light. Jesus came that we may have life and have it abundantly. Grace and peace of Jesus Christ through the Holy Spirit be with us as we continue this wondrous journey of faith in covenant with God and neighbor.

I am no longer my own, but thine.
Put me to what thou wilt, rank me with whom thou wilt.
Put me to doing, put me to suffering.
Let me be employed for thee or laid aside for thee,
exalted for thee or brought low for thee.
Let me be full, let me be empty.
Let me have all things, let me have nothing.
I freely and heartily yield all things to thy pleasure and disposal.
And now, O glorious and blessed God, Father, Son and Holy Spirit,
thou art mine, and I am thine.
So be it.
And the covenant which I have made on earth,
let it be ratified in heaven.
Amen. [4]

---

[4] As used in the Book of Offices of the British Methodist Church, 1936

Rev. Dr. Laceye Warner serves as the Royce and Jane Reynolds Associate Professor of the Practice of Evangelism and Methodist Studies and associate dean of Wesleyan engagement and hybrid learning at Duke Divinity School. As an ordained minister in the United Methodist Church, Dr. Warner continues to serve the denomination in a number of capacities including an elected delegate from the Texas Conference to General and Jurisdictional Conferences in 2016, 2019, and 2020.

Dr. Warner's *The Method of Our Mission: United Methodist Polity and Organization,* published by Abingdon Press in 2014, is a widely used and recognized textbook among United Methodist seminary students. In 2018 she co-authored with her husband From *Relief to Empowerment: How Your Church Can Cultivate Sustainable Mission* with Foundery Books.

She recently completed a 2021 Advent Study published by Abingdon Press, *All the Good: A Wesleyan Way of Advent,* as lead contributor with authors Jung Choi, Sangwoo Kim, and Amy Valdez-Barker.

CHAPTER THREE
Deciding the Future of Methodism:
It's Not Just About General Conference

William B. Lawrence

Introduction

The United Methodist Church, like all forms of Methodism, traces its founding to the Wesleyan movement in eighteenth-century England.[1] It is one of many denominations that grew from those roots and from schisms in the context of North American culture, politics, and racism.

The denominations with the longest institutional continuity in American Methodism are Black churches. The African Methodist Episcopal Church (AME) was founded in 1816, and the African Methodist Episcopal Zion Church (AMEZ) was founded in 1821. Several decades later, the Christian (originally "Colored") Methodist Episcopal Church (CME) was founded in 1870.

The mainly White Methodism known to most Americans has a history of institutional discontinuity with many schisms. Among the predominantly White denominations of American Methodists, the Wesleyans (1843) and Free Methodists (1860) endure longest, having formed as the result of disputes over slavery and governance. Governance, too, was the issue that led to the Methodist Protestant Church (MPC) in 1830, and slavery split northern and southern Methodists into separate denominations (MEC and MECS) in 1844. Those churches lasted a century until an MEC-MECS-MPC reunion in 1939. But "The Methodist Church" lasted just three decades. Its merger with the Evangelical United

---

[1] *The Book of Discipline of The United Methodist Church 2016*, United Methodist Publishing House).

Brethren in 1968 formed "The United Methodist Church."

So, American Methodism – from Wesley's movement in the eighteenth century to the present – has a history that is filled with institutional transitions. Schisms have happened often.

Now, after existing for a little more than five decades, The United Methodist Church is in jeopardy of coming apart. Some sort of splitting or splintering over human sexuality seems very likely. But who or what has the authority to decide the future of "United" Methodism?

Forces Besides Church Laws

Legislative proposals for divisions have been submitted to the next session of the General Conference. They include, but are not limited to, a widely discussed "protocol" for achieving the disunity of The United Methodist Church. Whether any such plan will be approved, when the often-postponed 2020 General Conference meets in 2024, is uncertain. Whether a plan that may be approved would require amending or rewriting the Constitution of The United Methodist Church is to be determined. Whether any action by the General Conference would be sufficient, on its own, to craft a tidy division of the denomination is doubtful.

So, it is unrealistic to predict what new form or forms of Methodism will be produced by further fractures. Forces other than constitutional order and legislative enactments are exerting pressure. *Ad hoc* groups appear to have powerful voices amid all the ecclesiastical noise.

Factors besides General Conference legislation could decide the future of an "untied" Methodism. Three such forces are discussed here: attrition, disconnection, and nullification.

Attrition

The United Methodist Church has been losing members ever since it began. Its founding event at a Uniting Conference in Dallas to celebrate the 1968 merger of the Evangelical United Brethren and The Methodist Church was its high-water mark in membership.

The authors of the chapters in this book could fill another one with discussions of reasons for the decline. They might include flawed decisions to redefine ministries, redirect budgets, and revise priorities. They might also include some shallow spirituality, theological immaturity, and unimaginative leadership during the decline. But attendance shrank, the average age of members rose, and people departed or simply drifted toward inactivity. However, external forces, as well as internal decisions, drove the decline. And these external forces have flourished in a time of crisis.

For decades, increasing numbers of Americans have been choosing alternatives to the paths of spirituality offered by the church. Many have chosen no religious affiliation for their spiritual interests, if they have any spiritual interests at all. According to Pew Research Center data, in 15 years from 2007 through 2021, the percentage of American adults who affiliate with Christianity has declined from 78% of the population to 63%, while the percentage of the American people who identify with no religion has risen from 16% to 29%.[2] This means that a much larger percentage of Americans consider themselves "Nones" than consider themselves "Catholics." There are about 10 times as many "Nones" in the United States as there are "Methodists."

These data show that attrition is more than people drifting away from attending worship. Attrition is a force that motivates people to define their lives and seek direction without religious affiliations. The data show that a significant percentage of Americans feels none of their needs is met by religious institutions and none of their hopes benefits from religious organizations. For personal guidance, public activities, or political perspectives, they turn to places other than the church.

The pandemic that began early in 2020 provided an environment for attrition to increase. Despite their efforts to conduct worship, hold Bible studies, and have business meetings online, churches found that COVID-19 was a relentless force. One interdenominational group noted that, when in-person worship resumed, attendance was 20% of pre-COVID levels. People opted for other choices – not just for their time but also for their money. Data from "Giving Tuesday" in 2021 reports

[2] Gregory A. Smith, "About Three-in-Ten U. S. Adults Are Now Religiously Unaffiliated," Pew Research Center, December 14, 2021 (pewforum.org).

increases of 6% in the amounts given and the numbers of donors giving, compared to 2020.[3] But church revenues did not share in that growth. United Methodist giving declined and apportionment payments dropped by $1.9 million from the previous year.

At its meeting conducted online on December 1, 2021, the General Council on Finance and Administration of The United Methodist Church reported that slightly more than half of the apportioned amounts had been received from annual conferences by that date. In addition, GCFA revised its budget proposal for the next General Conference and will submit a recommendation to cut the denomination's financial plan by nearly 33%. The impact of proposed program budget cuts would be even greater, reducing by 37% the amounts that denominational agencies would have to spend on theological education, ecumenical work, justice ministries, and other items.[4]

The force of attrition is potent. When members and money leave, they may never return.

But attrition involves more than members fading away from participation and money not offered to the church. It means that people are actively choosing to direct energies and resources elsewhere.

Forces of attrition are offering other means to satisfy needs of the human spirit. They are numbing the sense that those needs exist at all. The prescription for fixing this situation has little, if any, relationship to future legislative action at a General Conference.

Disconnection

The General Conference can abet such forces, as it did in authorizing local churches to disaffiliate from the denomination. In a time-limited provision of church law enacted at the called session of the General Conference in February 2019, United Methodist congregations, "for reasons of conscience" regarding church laws about homosexuality,

---

[3] Jessica Browning, "Trends that Will Shape Philanthropy in 2022," The Giving Institute, December 16, 2021 (givinginstitute.org).

[4] Heather Hahn, "Church Exits, COVID Lead to Steep Budget Cuts," *United Methodist News Daily Digest*, December 3, 2021. It is possible that apportionment payments submitted after the results of year-end giving may increase the percentage of the budget supported by revenue to a higher level of income for 2021.

can use procedures to exit from the denomination while retaining their property and other assets.[5]

In brief, the General Conference opened the door for a local United Methodist Church to see its denominational affiliation as optional. Paragraph 2553 in the *Discipline*, of course, does not state that explicitly, and it has clear requirements. But it was enacted after a century of changes that gave congregations power, which Wesley's *connexion* never envisioned. The phrase "local church" first appeared in northern and southern *Disciplines* in the 1920s. The Methodist Church revised its *Doctrines and Discipline* in the 1940s to put the "local church" in a separate chapter.

The trend continued in United Methodism. Annual conferences decreased interactions by superintendents with local churches and let local churches function more independently. Since the creation of The United Methodist Church, *The Book of Discipline* has said, "It is primarily at the level of the local church that the church encounters the world."[6] The General Conference in 2000 elevated the local church to be "the most significant arena through which disciple-making occurs."[7] The United Methodist Church altered the source of sacramental authority, from receiving ordination to being appointed. One's local setting now provides sacramental authority.

Local churches devise their own structures of governance and priorities in mission. Local churches choose how, or whether, to fund programs in personal discipleship and public welfare, leaving those in poorest neighborhoods to address the greatest problems with the fewest resources. Local churches choose curriculum to educate adults, children, and youth without a focus on Methodist or Wesleyan theological priorities. Local churches study ethics or public policy without studying United Methodist

---

[5] Paragraph 2553, *The Book of Discipline of The United Methodist Church 2016*, 2019 Addendum. While much attention has been given to churches that are opposed to ordaining homosexuals being the congregations that may pursue disaffiliation, at least a few Bishops said they consider any request from such a local church to be out of order, on the grounds that current church laws already prohibit ordaining or appointing homosexuals to ministry. Paragraph 2553 will expire at the end of 2023, and it can only be revised or extended by action of the General Conference. If no legislative session convenes, or if one convenes but takes no action on the matter, this portion of church law will be void on January 1, 2024.

[6] *The Book of Discipline of The United Methodist Church 1968*, United Methodist Publishing House, 1968) ¶ 102. It has endured in each edition of the Discipline since then. Paragraph 201 in the 2016 Discipline contains the same statement.

[7] *The Book of Discipline of The United Methodist Church 2000*, ¶ 201.

The pastor, a seminarian appointed as a student pastor, replied that the requirement was impractical, saying, "We do not have two unrelated persons in this congregation!"

social principles on health care, immigration, or other matters.

The trajectory of American Methodism (specifically United Methodism) for a century has emphasized the congregation and de-emphasized the connection. It has become common practice to disaffiliate from the denomination theologically, culturally, and prophetically. In an adult class at a local church, one teacher quoted from the Social Principles that health care "is a basic human right" and that "it is a governmental responsibility to provide all citizens with health care."[8] An irate member of the class said each local church should vote on such statements. He did not want to debate the merits of the statements. He wanted them not to exist without congregational vote.

Congregationalism has overtaken connectionalism in United Methodism. Disconnection is not radical or revolutionary. It is a trend. The legislation enacted by the General Conference in 2019 to permit local church disaffiliation is just an expansion of a hundred years of changes.

There are many ways that disconnection occurs. Some clergy and congregations boldly act to disconnect. At times, the connection is complicit in disconnecting. If a pastor practices rebaptism and the annual conference takes no disciplinary action,[9] the conference is complicit.

In one congregation, whose pastor was accused of sexual misconduct, a large portion of the membership opposed the authority of the conference to deal with the allegations, protect the accuser, and adjudicate the matter. The pastor was allowed by the annual conference to retire. Then, he launched an independent congregation that drew members from his former church.

In another congregation, a pastor announced he was leaving the

---

[8] See "Social Principles," Section III, "The Social Community," *The Book of Discipline of The United Methodist Church 2016,* ¶ 162.

[9] *The Book of Discipline of The United Methodist Church 2016,* ¶ 216.2b.

denomination and inviting members to leave with him. When the bishop told him he could not use the building, for it would belong to the annual conference, he said that the conference would also own its debt. In time, the members of the church who had remained could not manage to repay the indebtedness. To cover it, they sold the building at a discounted price to the former pastor's new church.

Most disconnections occur without such organizational drama. Pastors and lay members, with eclectic spiritualities and independent ecclesiologies, detach from Wesleyan theological foundations and Methodist connectional practices. Some say in first person singular, "my local church." Some bishops favor their areas but forget the earth in which they itinerate,[10] as on issues of race. In 1954, eight bishops from the Southeastern Jurisdiction asked that the Council of Bishops say nothing about desegregating public schools.[11] Forces of disconnection have been powerful in the church far longer than the disaffiliation that church law now temporarily allows.

Nullification

Besides, the authority of the church can be nullified. A powerful force within The United Methodist Church can obviate the doctrines and the disciplines of the denomination by ignoring them or working around them without rewriting them. Nullification can occur when a doctrinal standard, a clause in the Constitution, or a church law is merely deemed irrelevant, inapplicable, or unenforceable. This Methodist practice has a long history.

I was raised in a small northeastern Pennsylvania community where members on both sides of my extended family belonged to the same little Methodist church. In fact, on a Sunday morning, a few extended families occupied most places in the pews. During my high school years, I was president of the youth group, which meant I attended meetings of the official board and the "quarterly" conference. One agenda item at each quarterly conference mandated that the district

---

[10] See the Constitution, Division Two, Section III, Restrictive Rules, Article III, published in *The Book of Discipline of The United Methodist Church 2016*, ¶ 19.

[11] Russell E. Richey, Kenneth E. Rowe, Jean Miller Schmidt, *The Methodist Experience in America: A Sourcebook* Abingdon, 2000, Volume II.

superintendent ask, "Are all the offerings counted by two unrelated persons?" The pastor, a seminarian appointed as a student pastor, replied that the requirement was impractical, saying, "We do not have two unrelated persons in this congregation!" So, our local church nullified it.

But there are forms of nullification that serve political, not practical, aims. They are now being exercised by opposing sides of the dispute over sexuality that is likely to split the church.

For example, the Iowa Annual Conference cabinet announced on December 3, 2021, that "pastors will be able to choose which weddings they officiate" and local churches "will be able to determine their own policy regarding weddings."[12] This statement nullifies paragraphs in the *Discipline* that outlaw weddings or other ceremonies celebrating same-sex unions, services that "shall not be conducted by our ministers and shall not be conducted in our churches." Further, church law considers such a violation by a minister to be a chargeable offense.[13]

While that kind of nullification infuriates those who favor existing church laws,[14] those laws they prefer are also acts of nullification. Church laws that restrict ministerial conduct in regard to same-sex marriages and pastoral care of same-sex couples nullify the constitutional authority of the annual conference. According to the Constitution, an annual conference controls "all matters relating to the character and conference relations of its clergy members," including any judicial proceedings or trials of those clergy members.[15] The Constitution supersedes law.

Yet nullification is so powerful because it has been so effectively practiced by so many. Advocates for various sides and interests are defining issues and deciding questions on behalf of the church. For two years, *ad hoc* groups have deftly nullified connectional authority by going around it. An *ad hoc* group wrote the "protocol" that attaches a cost of at least $26 million to its plan for dividing the denomination.

---

[12] "Leading Now and Into the Future," December 3, 2021, a Statement of Vision from the Appointive Cabinet, published by the Iowa Annual Conference (iaumc.org).

[13] *The Book of Discipline of The United Methodist Church 2016*, ¶¶ 341.6 and 2702.1(b).

[14] Thomas Lambrecht, "Iowa Cabinet Jumps the Gun," *Perspective*, December 10, 2021.

[15] See the Constitution, Division Two, Section VI, Article II, and Section III (Restrictive Rules), Article III, published in *The Book of Discipline of The United Methodist Church 2016* ¶¶ 33 and 19 respectively.

Another *ad hoc* group promised $30 million from United Methodists to aid the victims of sexual abuse by Boy Scout leaders.

The "protocol" has become a hinge on which the hopes of many United Methodists hang as they imagine entering a door to the future. Lauded enthusiastically, yet cautiously, in an article by Robert Joseph Phillips,[16] the protocol was drafted by 16 self-appointed clergy and laity. It is a combination of ecclesiastical principles and legislative proposals that could result in a costly division of the denomination that financially supports one or more breakaway bodies.

The "agreement" regarding a fund that has been proposed as part of the legal bankruptcy of the Boy Scouts was negotiated by an *ad hoc* group whose unidentified members ignored an open meetings law.[17] Their commitment led bishops and district superintendents to call special charge conferences, to determine what the charge conference members could know about the agreement, and to design a voting procedure that deferred to the decisions of the *ad hoc* group. Within the first month of 2022, three annual conferences were called into special sessions by their bishops to approve the disbursement of funds from unrestricted reserves. More annual conferences may take similar actions in special or regular sessions because an *ad hoc* group achieved an unprecedented release of funds by going around – and nullifying – the leadership oversight by the Council of Bishops, the insights of the denomination's general agencies, and critical questions from the members of annual conferences or charge conferences.

Such *ad hoc* efforts may effectively nullify the systems of authority in the denomination. But they cannot do so without the cooperation of those authorities. Authors of the "protocol" had no capacity to send it to General Conference in spring 2020, but three annual conferences called special sessions and used a somewhat obscure provision in the *Discipline*[18] to put the "protocol" on the agenda. Advocates of the Boy Scout fund got bishops to call special conference sessions.

---

[16] Robert Joseph Phillips, "Methodist Mitosis: Taming The 'Wicked Problem' of The United Methodist Church," *Methodist Review: A Journal of Wesleyan and Methodist Studies,* 2021 (www.methodistreview.org).

[17] *The Book of Discipline of The United Methodist Church 2016* ¶ 722.

[18] *The Book of Discipline of The United Methodist Church 2016* ¶ 507.6.

The Limited Authority of the General Conference

Paragraph 509 in the *Discipline* clearly states that no entity "has the authority to speak officially for The United Methodist Church, this right having been reserved exclusively to the General Conference under the Constitution."[19] Paragraph 718, to which it refers, sets limits on statements that can be made by *ad hoc* groups but, in doing so, uses language that seems to make even broader claims.

Organizations not officially related to the General Conference may take positions only in their own names and may not speak for a general agency or the denomination as a whole.[20]

Of course, those statements in paragraphs 509 and 718 of the *Discipline* were adopted by General Conference itself as a claim of its own authority. They are often invoked with an implication that the General Conference has the last word on ALL church matters. But that is simply not true.

The Judicial Council is "not officially related" to the General Conference. It is an entity with its own constitutional authority. Members of the Council are present for sessions of General Conference but only to convene on site as needed for a matter, and they have neither voice nor vote at General Conference. Yet the Judicial Council speaks for "the denomination as a whole" when it issues a decision or memorandum, and it can overturn an act of General Conference.

The Council of Bishops is "not officially related" to the General Conference in the sense that it, too, is a constitutionally separate entity. Yet it speaks for "the denomination as a whole" when it issues public pronouncements and sets dates for jurisdictional conferences to convene. Moreover, the individual Bishops speak "for the denomination as a whole" when they choose whether to refer or dismiss a complaint and when they fix the appointments of pastors.

The General Conference has the final word on legislation, including some legislation that relates in various ways to certain operations of other constitutionally established entities, as the Constitution[21] clearly

---

[19] *The Book of Discipline of The United Methodist Church 2016* ¶ 509.1.

[20] *The Book of Discipline of The United Methodist Church 2016* ¶¶ 718.

[21] Division Two, Section II, Article IV, published in *The Book of Discipline of The United Methodist Church 2016* as ¶ 16. See also Division Two, Section VIII, Article I (published as ¶ 42) and Division Four, Article II (published as ¶ 56.5), for example.

stipulates. But it does not have the final word on all church matters.

Each annual conference has the final word on "all matters related to the character and conference relations of its clergy members," under the Constitution,[22] deciding who are licensed or ordained as ministers for the entire church. Similarly, each jurisdictional conference has the final word on who is elected as bishop. The General Conference has no authority to overrule other constitutional authorities on such items.

The church Constitution establishes the entity with the final word to speak officially for The United Methodist Church on a wide variety of decisions. It distributes that authority across the connection.

In addition, the Constitution establishes restrictions on the General Conference, naming actions that the General Conference "shall not" take. Indeed, while the Constitution establishes authorities and defines their decision-making responsibilities, it is only the General Conference that the Constitution specifically restricts from taking certain actions by establishing what the General Conference cannot do. Division Two, Section II, Articles I-VI, restricts the General Conference from taking any action that would change the church's doctrinal standards, turn the episcopacy into something other than a globally itinerant body, revoke the General Rules, or eliminate the right of clergy and laity to a trial before a person is removed from membership.[23] These "Restrictive Rules" have been in Methodist constitutions since 1808.

If any law enacted by General Conference had the effect of removing a member from The United Methodist Church without respecting the right of that member to a trial, it would violate the Fourth Restrictive Rule. If any law enacted by the General Conference granted authority to members of an annual conference (other than those who are designated by the Constitution[24]) to vote on the conference relations of clergy members, it would amend what the Constitution says without adopting a constitutional amendment. If any law enacted by the General Conference granted authority for an annual conference to secede from the denomination, it would transgress a clause in the Constitution that

---

[22] See Division Two, Section VI, Article II, published in *The Book of Discipline of The United Methodist Church 2016* ¶ 33.

[23] Published in *The Book of Discipline of The United Methodist Church 2016*, ¶¶ 17-21.

[24] Division Two, Section VI, Article II, published in *The Book of Discipline of The United Methodist Church 2016* as ¶ 33.

gives the jurisdictional conferences the exclusive authority to determine boundaries of annual conferences in their jurisdictions.[25]

However, such things could occur. Actions by the General Conference have limits. But other forces exist, including some that are prepared to ignore those limitations.

Conclusion

Besides the attrition, disconnection, and nullification active in United Methodism now, there are constitutional limits on what the General Conference can do. It has final authority in some spheres of decision-making. But it does not have final authority in all church decisions.

In 1939, when "The Methodist Church" was formed, the new denomination legislatively affirmed opposition to ministers' use of tobacco and alcohol. Until 1968, The Methodist Church had in place a law mandating abstinence from alcoholic beverages and tobacco. To be licensed to preach, elected as a clergy member of an annual conference, or be ordained, one had to agree to abstain.[26] In many conferences, the agreement was in writing.

Yet in states whose annual conferences and local churches relied heavily on members and revenues connected to the tobacco industry, that church law was nullified by ignoring it. In North Carolina, for example, candidates for ministry had to agree to abstain from alcohol but were told to ignore the requirement regarding tobacco.

There are powerful forces shaping the future of United Methodism. And the legislative process, with all its complicated ecclesiastical politics, is only one of those forces. Whatever a General Conference session may enact will only be one element in a collision of those forces.

Church laws against homosexuality have done nothing to stem the tide of attrition. The rearrangements of ecclesiastical infrastructure have done little but reinforce disconnection. Anything enacted by the General Conference could be pointless in a culture of nullification.

At the very least, it is naïve to trust that General Conference actions

---

[25] Division Two, Section IV, Article V, published in *The Book of Discipline of The United Methodist Church 2016* as ¶ 27.4.

[26] *Doctrines and Discipline of The Methodist Church 1964*, The Methodist Publishing House, ¶ 306.6.

will cure all that ails The United Methodist Church. Deciding the future of Methodism is the responsibility borne by many more people called Methodists than will gather as General Conference delegates soon, or at any time to come. The clergy and laity of The United Methodist Church, not the legislative assembly that is one of the many constitutional authorities in this connectional denomination, will decide its future.

William B. Lawrence is an ordained elder in The United Methodist Church and a clergy member of the North Texas Annual Conference in the retired relationship. He was a pastor in New York, Pennsylvania, and Washington DC, in addition to serving as a district superintendent. About half of his active ministry was in appointments at academic institutions, including 14 years as dean of Perkins School of Theology at Southern Methodist University.

He is now professor emeritus of American Church History at Perkins and a research fellow at the Center for Studies in the Wesleyan Tradition at Duke Divinity School. He served a term on the Judicial Council and for four years was its president. He and his wife Naomi live in Chapel Hill, North Carolina.

CHAPTER FOUR
A New Thing

Kristin Joyner

There's an aged, faded, exhausted old red Ford sitting in the back lot. It was the hottest car when it first came out, people stopped and stared at the bright red power horse as it roared down the boulevard. Over the years, the car and its drivers had many experiences, some delightful and some dreadful.

When the children were younger the back seat was plenty spacious for the swinging feet, but as the legs grew longer, the kick prints scarred the fabric. The generous size was good for a while but eventually was difficult to fit into parking garages. The shiny right side was crunched against the corner of a concrete post and orange paint was used to cover the dent and scratches. The original bright headlights faded to a hazy yellow and cracks appeared as the lenses dulled. Exuberant drivers and careless passengers gradually wore down the upholstery and rugs, stories now marked by duct tape. The indicators of a lifetime were imprinted forever, the good and the bad.

The car still drives, the blinkers still blink and the brakes still brake. The rearview mirror broke off, although no one remembers why but a close-enough replacement was found at a junk yard. The V-8 greedily gulps gasoline, demanding short trips or a fat wallet for support. The old Ford rests quietly parked most of the time, contrary to its intended purpose. Leaves and pine needles collect in the crevices. No one stares in awe as it rumbles down the road anymore. It is still a car, but there are new ones, shinier ones, ones that don't guzzle fuel and have safety features – like seat belts that actually buckle, and air bags that save lives.

The new rides have features with options for music and storytelling, comforting air temperature controls, and are friendlier to the environment. They have guidance systems to assist in direction and allow congestion avoidance. Old faithful does have the ability to transport a person from one place to the next so the loyalists want to hang on to it, sinking in more money, time and mechanics. However, the time must come to say goodbye to the good and faithful Ford and to say hello to a new set of wheels.

New wheels now come in various forms. There are scooters and bikes to rent, mass transit and light rail in many cities, ride shares, taxis and drivers who are only a few clicks away. Individually owned vehicles aren't the only or best choice for many. It's time to acknowledge the evolution of safety, efficiency, guidance, even comfort. The signs are all there, green lighting the way for the long road still to come.

> *No one sews a piece of unshrunk cloth on an old cloak; otherwise, the patch pulls away from it, the new from the old, and a worse tear is made. And no one puts new wine into old wineskins; otherwise, the wine will burst the skins, and the wine is lost, and so are the skins; but one puts new wine into fresh wineskins.*

Mark 2:21-22 (NRSV)

It's time. The signs are all there.

We have had an uninvited opportunity in these past two years to create, and to be, the church in new and exciting ways. The pandemic has been called the "great revealer" in the way it has forced us to consider new ways of being; opening a door that we didn't know needed to be opened. This unexpected, unplanned opportunity beckons our participation. It has compelled us into new ways of being in community – and in being in connection, in expanding our methods and practices, in creativity! We have been called to become disciples and to create church in new ways, like new wine. This new wine cannot be put into old wineskins and we can't put the new cloth on the old cloak, or put one more piece of duct tape on the Ford.

It's time. The signs are all there.

In *Where Do We Go From Here: Honest Responses From Twenty-Four United Methodist Leaders,"*[1] many descriptors were used in response to the current state of the United Methodist Church (UMC). The church was described as a "broken body"[2] and a "defunct and clearly overburdened structure,"[3] that is "waging an internal war,"[4] that is now "famous for placing homosexuals on the margins,"[5] and that the UMC has become "a church that not only sanctions, but encourages, harm."[6] Even counter balancing those statements with the acknowledgement of the good that the church is doing, the indictments are clear. The UMC has become something it ought not to be.

The General Conference is the body that speaks for this denomination but sadly the descriptions of that body were also condemning. It was an "incendiary gathering"[7] where "debates raged"[8] and "there were no winners."[9] It was a "debacle,"[10] a "dumpster fire"[11] with "embarrassing acrimony."[12] The old body isn't working and the mouthpiece isn't either.

The most pronounced symptom of our inoperable current condition is the argument about LGBTQIA inclusion. This symptom is not the reason we are in the conversation about splitting our denomination. People who identify as LGBTQIA are not the problem. The problem isn't the debates about theology or scriptural obedience either. Debates have happened before. It's very likely that some people have left General Conference every year since inception on the losing side of a debate.

The power struggle that is occurring is because there is an imbalance of power within the structure of the church. We are arguing about power. This current debate is about how we function as followers of

---

[1]   Kevin Slimp, *Where Do We Go From Here? Honest Responses From Twenty-Four United Methodist Leaders,* Market Square Publishing, 2019.

[2]   Ibid. da Silva Souto, Alex, 45.

[3]   Ibid. da Silva Souto, Alex, 47.

[4]   Ibid. Farr, Bishop Bob, 84.

[5]   Ibid. Lawrence, William B., 118.

[6]   Ibid. Malachi, Laquaan, 132.

[7]   Ibid. Ritter, Chris, 166.

[8]   Ibid. Cantrell, Will, 19.

[9]   Ibid. Acevedo, Jorge, 6.

[10] Ibid. Meeks, M. Douglas, 137.

[11] Ibid. Farr, Bishop Bob Farr, 79.

[12] Ibid. Carder, Bishop Kenneth, 27.

Christ in a structure, and institution that holds power with a top-down, institutional hierarchy operating as regulator, not supporter, of the mission of the denomination. We are in a disagreement about whether or not we can disagree. The narrow majority made this very clear by approving increased disciplinary action by the bishops. Nearly half of the body, not a slim minority, disagreed with this significant message. Power and control were at work, not Holy discernment about who this denomination needs to continue to be in the world.

The conversations about remaining as one denomination seem to be waning. Even if there could be a resolution on the matter of who can and cannot be ordained or married, there is little hope that would be enough to keep us joined together. That is because the well-worn arguments about LGBTQIA inclusion are only signs and symptoms of our broken system. The tool we are using to solve this debate is either the wrong tool, or the tool is wrong. The state of our denomination right now is an argument about what kind of a system we are called to be part of and participate in. Some want to be in a system that allows differences, some want to be in a system that does not. We are scrapping together and adding discipline to a book regulating who has power and who doesn't, who can have jobs and who can't, who can maintain financial health and who will suffer.

Disagreement is hard. Losing power is hard. Giving up control is hard, but prioritizing control over those who are harmed by it is not the call of any part of the church. We cannot prioritize saving an institution over saving the actual work of Jesus and the people whom God loves.

We have let the focus of our denomination become about institution and discipline and not about the mission given to us by Jesus Christ.

The purpose of the church comes from scripture, from tradition and from the experience and reasons that we have in each unique context. The church should lead all towards grace, love of God and love of neighbor. We do this not as volunteers and humanitarians, but as seekers of God's presence and joiners of God's work. In the words of Bishop Carder, this is found "in identification with the poor, the oppressed, the excluded, the pushed aside, the abused, the powerless, the scorned. There is where God is most clearly, radically, redemptively and transformatively present!"[13]

---

[13] Bishop Kenneth L. Carder, "The Way Forward: Repentance and Confession," in *Where Do We Go From Here? Honest Responses From Twenty-Four United Methodist Leaders*, ed. Kevin Slimp, Market Square Publishing, 2019.

The rules and laws we follow should support and encourage us, and not become barriers and interference. To understand our outmoded system is to understand where we should go next.

I love the potential of the church.

I am dismayed by the amount of staff time, laity time, angst, hurt, financial assets and administrative resources that have been exhausted trying to define what the United Methodist Church thinks about homosexuality. Fundamentally that argument translates into limiting who someone can love. If this denomination is arguing for less love in the world, then we are worse off than we think. It would make sense if we were discussing something that creates victims or begets violence, but that's not what we're doing. Both sides of this argument are saying they are in obedience to scripture and no human or legislation is going to change their stance.

Because just as Peter and the apostles said,
"We must obey God rather than any human authority."

Acts 5:29 (NRSV)

In our current example, we disagree over what it means to obey God. Scripture isn't clear enough to be clear universally – if it was, God-fearing, God-loving, educated people wouldn't have disagreements regarding interpretation. This is why the UMC created governing documents.

The Book of Discipline was first created in 1784 to explain clergy roles, salaries and sacraments and has been modified and duct-taped ever since. The book includes chargeable offenses and trials, hierarchy and judicial systems. This governance system was being developed at relatively the same time our own United States governance was forming and growing. Roberts rules, democratic process, delegations and memberships are kin to the American governance system. It wasn't set up with global perspectives or cultural understandings. The structure of it was meant to be "more specific and less open to interpretation so Methodists across the entire continent could function as one coordinated body."[14] Of course

---

[14] "When was the first Book of Discipline created?", The United Methodist Church, accessed January 21, 2022, https://www.umc.org/en/content/ask-the-umc-when-was-the-first-book-of-discipline-created.

as the denomination grew, acknowledgement of necessary differences in the structures of U.S. conferences and the Central Conference were added. There are limits to the Central Conference to "promote the evangelistic, educational, missionary, social concern and benevolent interests and institutions of the church within their own boundaries."[15] Thus an example of an acknowledgement that boundaries do exist and we recognize that even through connection, we do some things according to each context. This is why adding, changing, and keeping old systems and structures begins to feel like orange paint patches on an old red Ford.

As a denomination, it is necessary to remember that we are also part of an even bigger global church, the body of Christ, an extension of Christ's life and ministry in the world today.[16] Our journey to perfection and unity in all things essential began a long time ago and so did the splitting up of the body into denominations. We have splintered and fragmented, bandaged and reformed since the church began.

The United Methodist Church is not the first or last victim in this long history of church breakups. The vision of a "big tent" United Methodist Church always has excluded most of the church – the part of the body that wasn't United Methodist. We can grieve that the UMC is dividing, but it is merged with the grief that the church is already divided into thousands of smaller churches, each bearing gifts and sins of their own. Focusing the complete mission of Jesus Christ and God's vision on ourselves is also a sin. If the UMC ceases to exist, there will be absorption and distribution of people into the truly global church. The mission of the church won't fall apart. Why? Because the United Methodists are not the only part of the body seeking the transformation of the world or mercy, charity, grace and justice.

We must have more confidence in God. God will continue to show up in ways that we haven't planned for and are likely impeding.

When our fighting and disagreements come to impasse and our governance and disciplines can't solve our problems, it is time for

---

[15] "Book of Discipline, 2016 online. Paragraph 3", Cokesbury, accessed January 21, 2011, https://www.cokesbury.com/book-of-discipline-book-of-resolutions-free-versions.

[16] "Our Christian Beliefs: The Church", The United Methodist Church, accessed January 21, 2022, https://www.umc.org/en/content/our-christian-roots-the-church.

something new. The pandemic has taught us many difficult lessons and everyone will lose out if we don't take this opening to co-create new wine. Local churches are ministering to the world in contexts that aren't solely geographic. Mission, service and study are forever changed through technology, reach and connection. Sacraments, singing, worship, prayer and offering are accessible in new and exciting ways. Churches' property and buildings are underutilized resources yet to fulfill their utmost purpose. The opportunity for boldness to follow God is upon us now.

Where do we go from here?

Usher in a new wine with a new wineskin. The conversation about creating new denominations arose without asking if the world actually needs more denominations, but I don't think we will argue about a world needing vibrant local churches. In the U.S., we know that there is a rapid decline in trusting institutions. It's a longshot to believe that new denominations can be created that will answer the cries in the U.S., let alone the world. To create trustworthy institutional authority would require starting with the local churches and the communities in which they serve – communities that may be international, global, online, or that may be concentrated, intensely local, even isolated. Build a denomination, or one part of the church from the ground up, not the institution down. From the ashes of a deceased denomination, new life can rise up and dance!

To hold the dearly beloved Methodist traditions and legacy together until new creations arise, will mean redefining some of the structures, elements and systems that have been valued for decades.

- We honor the good of the past, acknowledge and repent of our sins, grieve where we must and then go on a path that redistributes our part of the Body, forming trust and discipleship-making more locally.

- Make smaller the structures that oversee, not re-using old terms but coming up with fresh designations.

- Perhaps our communions are based on geography at first, separated by country or continent for common cultural and legal reasons, but likely serving with and for people from any worldwide location.

- Commit to a just tithe of financial support in a way that distributes to each as any have needs.

- Support models that encourage the agencies to be successful as non-profits with their unique missions for relief, curriculum and communications.

- Update our commitment to and understanding of connection. Characterize connection as being intentional about not isolating ourselves, especially connection with those who have different experiences and cultures.

- Maintain connections to the global family through something like the World Methodist Council with a biennial or quadrennial meeting of all the Wesley family, for purposes other than authority and governance.

- Consider as a model how we respect our alliances with our interfaith partners, where we honor their understanding of God in our listening, care and support. We can find deep connections through differences without weakening our own identities in faith. Identify as one part of the larger body of Christ, in unity through grace.

The signs are there, the opportunity is before us. May those who are called lead us into a new thing, like new wine with a new wineskin. Thanks be to God that we are loved because of who God is, not because of who we are.

Rev. Kristin Joyner is an ordained deacon serving as Pastor of Community Engagement at Bothell United Methodist Church in Washington State. She is called to connect the life of the community with the life of the congregation, blurring the lines and evolving the definition of both. Her passion is in making sure people have access to homes and housing that is affordable.

Kristin is an author and contributor to two books, *Stories of the Congo,* published by the PNW Conference and *Filling the Void, Voices from the None Zone,* Market Square Publishing.

CHAPTER FIVE
A New Visionary Future

Kay Kotan

If people can't see what God is doing,
they stumble all over themselves;
But when they attend to what he reveals,
they are most blessed.

Proverbs 29:18 MSG

According to Incus Services, a vision is a guiding force that keeps your organization focused on its goals, mission, objectives, or what you want to accomplish. It's about how you see the world around you as well as how others should see it, too. Without having a clear sense of direction, organizations can easily go astray without even realizing it.[1]

What is the vision of the United Methodist Church? Is our vision to avoid or survive a schism? Is our vision to try to hang on to what remains of the United Methodist Church? Or, as Proverbs suggests, are we stumbling all over ourselves because we don't have a vision and can't see what God is doing?

New Vision and Leadership

While most leaders in the UMC could agree that the church is about making disciples (our mission), I would guess that most would not have a common understanding of what that looks like or how to measure the effectiveness of doing so. Even worse, there has been no vision cast for where the United Methodist Church is headed. There is no guiding

---

[1] https://incusservices.com/why-vision-is-important-in-business-management-and-leadership/.

path for where we are headed. We lack a sense of direction. We have no shared guidance leading the church into God's preferred future. While some have a realistic view of the current culture, I fear that many who sit in our pews have an unrealistic understanding of the contemporary postmodern culture and how to reach them.

In a *Harvard Business Review,* Tony Mayo provided some insights regarding the importance of vision: "The ability to visualize and articulate a possible future state for an organization has always been a vital component of successful leadership. The downfall of many a failed (leader) has also been attributed to their lack of vision. Vision divorced from context can produce very erratic and unpredictable results. Great leaders need to walk the fine line between capitalizing on the opportunities ripe for the present context and planning for a possible future state. Leaders can shape the parameters for success through a vision for the future. And, just as important, they possess the ability to oversee that vision's implementation."[2]

Because of the structure of the UMC, who would be responsible for casting a vision to guide us into the next chapter of our future? Who would create the vision's implementation plan and oversee it? Does that responsibility and authority rest with the bishops? The Connectional Table? As stated in my latest book, *A Cry From the Pew,* the complexity of our structure in the UMC makes it challenging to understand and navigate where this type of critical and holy work would take place, let alone who is responsible and accountable. In addition, the complexity of the structure also makes the timeliness of such a process cumbersome and nearly impossible.

New Vision for Such a Time as This

> *Forget about what's happened;*
> *don't keep going over old history.*
> *Be alert, be present.*
> *I'm about to do something brand-new.*
> *It's bursting out! Don't you see it?*

Isaiah 43:19-21 MSG

---

[2] Tony Mayo, "The Importance of Vision," *Harvard Business Review,* October 29, 2007, https://hbr.org/2007/10/the-importance-of-vision.

There is no doubt our world has dramatically changed since March 2020. It will be years, if not a decade or more, before we realize the full effects of the pandemic and the resulting endemic. For the church, the pandemic exacerbated the conditions already present in the church. For example, if the church was already in decline, the decline likely accelerated more significantly during the pandemic. In contrast, a church that was deeply connected to the community and growing likely continued to grow through the pandemic and did so at an accelerated pace. Some estimate that the accelerant effect for the church during the pandemic was equivalent to a "normal" 10-year period.

One of the most exciting things that happened during the pandemic was disruption. Admittedly some disruption caused chaos and worse, but the church also had the opportunity to capitalize on this disruption if it chose to do so. As Albert Einstein once said, "In every crisis lies great opportunity," so often in the life of the church, it is difficult to stop precious programs or bury out-lived ineffective ministries or retire worn-out events. The pandemic disrupted everything and gifted us with the opportunity to reevaluate everything at the local level, the district level, the annual conference level, and the general church level. Unfortunately, too many rushed back to Egypt trying to recapture a sense of comfort and "normalcy" and missed this precious window of opportunity.

God uses all things for good - including a pandemic. How did your local church respond? How did your annual conference respond? How did the general church respond? Did we keep our eyes wide open? Did we pray and discern God's preferred future? Did we seek to discern the needs or the problems to be solved for our community? Were we fully present? Were we alert? Were we more focused on our own desires and personal preferences than God's guidance and the community's needs?

As we think about the upcoming General Conference (whenever that might commence), where is the opportunity in this disruption? I believe God is doing a new thing. The church in the United States is losing ground. A growing number of people are unchurched, de-churched, none, and done. Maybe we are here for such a time as this to be bold and courageous to follow God's lead to do a new thing. New things normally start from the fringes - not from the center or the institutions. Is God calling us to a new movement? Or, at the very least, is God calling us for a major restructuring, simplification, and a new vision to reach new people in a new way?[3]

If we don't want to kick the can down the alley once again or spend the next several decades tweaking the *Book of Discipline* into a workable postmodern polity, we have to see this as a disruption ripe with opportunity. But we have to set aside all of the special interest groups' agendas and truly discern God's preferred future for the UMC - not our own! To do that we have to make sure we are poised and ready to truly listen to God. Are our eyes wide open? Are we praying and discerning guidance for God's preferred future for the UMC? Are we paying attention to how we need to show up as the church to reach those who have yet to know Jesus Christ? Are we fully present? Are we alert? Are we paying attention beyond our personal desires and personal agendas? How is God whispering in our ear?

New Vision in the Local Mission Field

Regardless of what happens at the general church level, the local church is where disciples are developed and where disciple-makers reach new people for Kingdom impact. This will not change! However, being a Christian is now being a minority. Where Christians were once the majority of the population, this is no longer the case in the postmodern world. This means the way we did church previously is no longer sufficient nor effective to reach new people. Most people will not wake up on Sunday and decide to go try out a church for the first time. Not only is it not on their minds – it is not even on their radar! There are now up to three non-churched generations.

Due to the cultural shifts accelerated by the pandemic, the church will need to pay attention to some major shifts in their focus and how they engage in the communities. The church needs to become less building centric, less Sunday centric, and less in-person centric. Instead, the church needs to become more community and relationally centric as well as leadership equipper and spiritual entrepreneur. Let

---

[3] *A Cry From the Pew,* Market Square Publishing, 2022.

me briefly unpack each of these here, but you can also find out more at CreationIncubator.org.

If the pandemic helped the church realize nothing else, it reminded us that the church is not a particular building we go to on a particular day at a particular time. The church is a movement of people on mission for Jesus Christ. Yet so often we use so much of our resources (time, energy, money) to care for and preserve our facilities. It is often the church's largest asset and expense. We need to rethink how to leverage this asset for the mission of making disciples. This is not about becoming a landlord! No, it is about *leveraging* for the *mission*. What poor stewardship to use the Lord's building for only an hour or two a week!

Another lesson the pandemic has taught us is that people appreciate worship at times other than on Sunday and in-person. Often the downloads throughout the week far exceed the views for worship viewed on Sunday live or the number of people attending in-person worship. People appreciate the flexibility of participating in worship when it fits their schedule. Not everyone can travel to a building. Some have sensory issues personally or their children do. Some feel more comfortable experiencing worship in the safety of their own space. We also need to get past only thinking of online worship and expand our thinking to offering a comprehensive online ministry. Read more about this in *Being the Church in the Post Pandemic World.*

One of the areas we need to focus on more is being more relationally and community-centric. People are looking for a sense of belonging and a place to be a part of a community. They are not looking for a friendly church; they are looking for friendships that are authentic and transparent. They are looking for a safe place where it is okay to ask questions and not be told what to believe, but be able to form their own thoughts, ideas, and opinions. As the church, we should be better at this than any other organization! But to be this type of safe-haven for the community, we must be community-centric rather than inwardly focused on those that are already gathered as part of the church's congregation. We must be hyper-focused on what is going on in the community and how the church collectively and how we individually as Christians are weaved into the tapestry of the community. We must become part of the heartbeat of the community. We meet our neighbors where they are; we don't expect them to come to us (spiritually, physically, and metaphorically).

Another area we need to focus on more is moving from being more shepherd-led to be instead more focused on being equippers of leaders and spiritual entrepreneurs. Our heritage was a laity movement that was much less pastor-centric. When our movement was more laity-led, we were a growing movement. We need to return to those roots and encourage, equip, and release laity for ministry. One of the ways we can do this is through marketplace multipliers. Laity spend most of their time in the marketplace – their jobs, the gym, grocery store, ball fields, parks, shopping, etc. Helping laity feel equipped and comfortable integrating their faith and their work/daily lives by seeing the marketplace's potential to be the place where the opportunity for people to establish a relationship with Jesus through the example and influence found in the relationships they develop in daily environments. For more information, check out MarketplaceMultipliers.org and *Expanding the Reach Through Marketplace Multipliers*.[4]

Another way we can become leadership equippers is to fully lean into the purpose of the Committee on Nominations. The full name of this committee is Committee on Nominations and Leadership Development. Yes, this committee is responsible for raising and equipping leaders in the church. Where the church was once the place where leaders were developed, the church now expects the secular world to raise up leaders and send them to the church to lead. What is your leadership development process in your local church? This includes leaders not only for the administrative committees (trustees, finance, SPRC, Council), but this also includes ministry team leaders, youth leaders, small group leaders, staff, etc. What kind of budget do you have for leadership development? If you do not have a leadership development process, check out these resources: *Launching Leaders*,[5] *Church Ecology*,[6] *and Equipping Lay Venture Leaders*.[7]

Finally, another focus we need to shift is being more of a spiritual

---

4   Schmidt, Whitcher & Kotan, *Expanding the Reach Through Marketplace Multipliers*, Market Square Publishing, 2021.

5   Kay Kotan & Phil Schroeder, *Launching Leaders*, Market Square Publishing, 2019.

6   Willard & Brown, Church Ecology: Creating a Leadership Pathway for Your Church, Market Square Publishing, 2020.

7   Kelly Brown, Equipping Lay Venture Leaders, Market Square Publishing, 2021.

entrepreneur as a church and as individual leaders. Again, this is part of our heritage, but we have moved away from it. It is time for us to reclaim these vital roots. We once were the ones who founded schools, hospitals, and orphanages. Now, so many churches are reluctant to do anything other than "church." Helping people and communities survive and strive is at the very core of who we are as Christians and United Methodists. To leverage our assets, whether it is our dollars, facilities, energy, expertise, experience, time, equipment, grounds, commercial kitchen, or vehicles, *is being* the church! We have to move past simply donating items and become more relationally-centric in our leveraging our assets to meet needs, solve problems, build new relationships, and make our community a better place to raise families and build businesses. When we become relationally and community-centric, discipleship deepens, and new people become disciples. When a church is inwardly focused on those already gathered, discipleship *might* deepen (although one could argue that mature disciples recognize their responsibility and honor to disciple others). However, it is doubtful new people will become disciples, and the church will decline (or decline faster).

New Vision: A Call to Something More

A vision is not just a picture of what could be;
it is an appeal to our better selves,
a call to become something more.

Rosabeth Moss Kanter

This is not about saving the United Methodist Church! Being a fourth-generation United Methodist, that is difficult to say. It is so much more. God is up to something new. Something big. Something more. Something that we can probably not even yet imagine. It may or may not occur in our lifetime. But we are here now to do our part right now.

We have placed limitations on what the church is, what the church does, what the church stands for, what the church stands against, and what the church is to be. We have gotten in our own way. We have gotten in God's way. We need to surrender to God's will. We need to surrender to God's preferred future. We need to release all limitations of what we think the church can do, can't do, is about, and isn't about. God is on the move!

We are being called into a new vision of God's preferred future.

We are being called into a better version of being the church!

We are being called into something much more!

Won't you join me in prayer for discerning a new vision?

Kay Kotan is the founder of *You Unlimited*. She is also the founder of *The Greatest Expedition* (greatestexpedition.com), a collaboration of more than twenty thought leaders providing resources and insights for a congregational journey to develop new ministry action plans to reach new people.

As a passionate lay person, she has a banking background and has been a business owner for more than 25 years. Kotan has served as a church developer for conferences and worked with churches, pastors, conferences, and judicatory leaders across the country for more than a decade.

Her most recent best-sellers include *Being the Church in a Post-Pandemic World* (Market Square Books), *Mission Possible 3+* (Market Square Books), and *Cry From the Pews* (Market Square Books).

CHAPTER SIX
Shifting the Margins

Bishop Kenneth L. Carder

"The Spirit of the Lord is upon me,
because he has anointed me
to bring good news to the poor.
He has sent me to proclaim release to the captives
and recovery of sight to the blind,
to let the oppressed go free,
to proclaim the year of the Lord's favor."

Luke 4:18-19 (NRSV)

Methodism stands at the crossroads. We've been here before.

As a movement, Methodism was birthed at the crossroads and has been reborn multiple times over more than three centuries of life-determining responses to "What's next?" Fresh from his heartwarming experience at Aldersgate Street on May 24, 1738, John Wesley faced a crossroads when invited by George Whitefield to move outside the formality of his Anglican comfort zone and proclaim the gospel to the poor in the open air.

A case can be made that April 2, 1739, marked the date when John Wesley took the decisive step in birthing the Methodist movement. He went to the margins of 18th-century England, preached to the working poor at Bristol, thereby launching a revival that spread across the British Empire and the American frontier. He intentionally shifted the center of his life and ministry to those whom Jesus called "the least of these" (Matthew 25:31-45), and Charles Wesley referred to as "Jesus' bosom friends," the working poor, the imprisoned, the sick, the outcast and pushed aside.[1]

Wesley spent the next half-century in relationship and ministry with those on the margins of polite and privileged English society. He ate their food, stayed in their modest homes when traveling, caught their diseases, collected money for their aid, started schools to educate their children and medical clinics to treat their sicknesses. He developed cooperatives in response to the need for employment and a lending agency to provide economic assistance. The poor were far more than objects of Wesley's charity; they were his friends, co-workers, and colleagues.

Those on the margins of society were the center of early Methodism's life and mission. They were members and leaders of classes and bands and full participants in the preaching, teaching, and administrative functioning of the Methodist Societies and structures. Early Methodism was a movement of the poor, with the poor, and for the poor. I am convinced they helped shape John Wesley's overarching message and experience of grace, the presence and power of God to reconcile and transform human hearts, communities, nations, and the entire cosmos.

Over the last three centuries, Methodism has struggled with who occupies the center of its nature and mission and who are relegated to the margins. Wesley himself lived with that tension, especially later in his life. In his 80s, he toured the Methodist Societies across the British Isles and returned discouraged. The Methodists were becoming prosperous and drifting away from their presence among the poor and society's marginalized. He felt that as their wealth and privilege increased, their experience of the saving, energizing, and transforming power of divine grace was decreasing. He warned that the Methodists were thereby in danger of becoming a "dead sect, having the form of religion without the power."[2]

---

[1] For a thorough analysis of Wesley's involvement with the poor and the role the poor played in the formation of Methodism, read Theodore W. Jennings, *Good News to the Poor: John Wesley's Evangelical Economics* Abingdon Press, 1990; M. Douglas Meeks, Editor, *The Portion of the Poor: Good News to the Poor in the Wesleyan Tradition*, Kingswood Books, 1995; and Richard P. Heitzenrater, *The Poor and the People Called Methodist*, Abingdon Press, 2002). *Portion of the Poor* is a collection of the lectures delivered at the Ninth Oxford Institute of Methodist Theological Studies in 1992.

[2] "Thoughts Upon Methodism," dated August 4, 1786, *Wesley's Works*, Baker Book House, 1872 edition. For additional expressions of Wesley's concern about the impact of losing relationships with the poor see these sermons, "Causes of the Inefficacy of Christianity," "On God's Vineyard," and "The Use of Money."

The current crisis confronting The United Methodist Church, especially in the United States, is but the latest manifestation of the tension over who occupies the center of the church's life and mission and who is relegated to the margins. It matters mightily:

- who is included and who is excluded
- who is at the center of the decisions and who is on the periphery
- whose voices are magnified and who is silenced
- who is visible and who is hidden
- who has the power, and who is rendered powerless.

The contemporary United Methodist Church can recover its presence among the poor, the vulnerable, the powerless, and the forgotten who are at the center of the Triune God's life and mission. It will require learning from the mistakes of the past, reordering priorities, and intentionally shifting the margins of the denomination's composition, mission, and practices.

The Shift to Respectability and Privilege

The tension John Wesley experienced and wrote about – as Methodists became more prosperous – intensified in the American context. By the middle of the 19th century, Methodism had become the dominant denomination and wielded significant social and political power. Numerical growth became the measure of evangelization and fueled a sense of optimism and divine providence. The gospel of personal salvation and freedom of the will fit well into the cultural values of individualism, capitalism, free market, and personal autonomy. The episcopal/connectional polity allowed for the deployment of circuit riders where populations were moving and provided structures for mission.

Through the strong influence of leaders such as Nathan Bangs and Bishop Matthew Simpson, Methodism intentionally and strategically turned toward reaching the "weightier" people.[3] Respectability, upward mobility, social and political prestige became prominent values. Plain

---

[3] See Nathan Hatch, *The Democratization of Christianity*, Yale University Press, 1989, especially chapter 7.

preaching houses located on back streets gave way to more ornate structures on main streets. Circuit riders began dismounting their horses to become "stationed" pastors. Theological training and higher education designed to equip pastors to appeal to the more educated grew in importance and expectation. The cultivation of political influence occupied many bishops and prominent pastors, and Methodists became the leading denomination in state and national governments. Colleges and universities were founded and funded, and Christian education with standardized curriculum gradually replaced camp meetings and revivals as primary institutions for Christian initiation and nurture.

The Methodist emphasis on individualism, freedom of will, and personal salvation resonated with American values of individual liberty, personal liberty, and upward social mobility. The dramatic numerical growth and social and political prominence resulted in Methodism becoming the quintessential religious organization throughout 19th-century America. Historian Nathan Hatch described foundational American Methodism as follows:

Methodism resonated with the logic of capitalism and liberal individualism...it is the meteoric rise of American Methodism that offers insight into a society that was awash in religion and making money – and confident of divine favor upon both endeavors. American Methodism was the prototype of a religious organization taking on market form.[4]

Methodism's growth in respectability, political prominence, and institutional strength during the 19th and early 20th centuries resulted in many praiseworthy advancements of the church's mission. The founding of colleges and universities, health and welfare institutions, and the growth of Christian education curriculum and institutes contributed greatly to society and the church's mission. Thousands and millions of people were converted to the Christian faith and formed in discipleship. An expansive foreign missions effort resulted in widespread educational, medical, agricultural, and evangelistic ministries across the globe. Methodists provided valuable leadership in business, education, government, and countless philanthropic institutions.

By the mid-20th century, the Methodist shift from the poor to the

---

[4] Nathan O. Hatch, "The Puzzle of American Methodism," in John H. Wigger, Nathan O. Hatch, editors, Methodism in the Shaping of American Culture, Kingswood Books, 2001.

prosperous and privileged had been completed, creating unintended consequences along the way. The market logic of success as upward social mobility, institutional dominance, and political prestige and prominence now dominates The United Methodist Church in the United States, separating us from our own Wesleyan roots among "the least of these" where Jesus clearly declares we are called to be.

Dangers of the Market-Formed Church

Wesley's warning of the dangers of wealth and loss of community with the poor reached full expression in the American context. In his sermons, Wesley warned that increased wealth and its privileges tended to diminish reliance on and experience of transforming grace. Methodism not only took on "market form," it bought into the market *logic* of consumerism, growth, and commodification. Evangelism became synonymous with church growth, resulting in compromising on fundamental moral foundations such as the dignity of ALL persons, including enslaved people, on behalf of institutional growth. In a market consumerist culture, worship becomes a marketing strategy for attracting the masses. Leadership is defined as institutional management. The gospel itself becomes another commodity to be sold in the marketplace of ideas. Ordained ministry dissolves into a profession available to the highest bidders, the congregations with the most wealth. In a market-formed church, the God of the Exodus and of the crucified and risen Christ becomes unnecessary, maybe even a hindrance. All that is needed is a popularly derived strategic plan and a clever marketing campaign.

When statistical growth of the institutional church becomes the measure of faithfulness and the effectiveness of evangelization, the church becomes a "dead sect, having the form of religion without the power." The deadly consequence of the shift from the logic of grace to the logic of market consumerism is most tragically evident in the Methodist Church's long-standing struggle with race. Wesley's uncompromising anti-slavery stance was quickly compromised within a quadrennium of the formation of The Methodist Episcopal Church in 1784. One church historian affirmed that Methodism's moral authority began its decline when, in the name of church growth, it softened the stance on slavery.[5] The formation of the Central Jurisdiction in 1939 was a further compromise of the gospel on behalf of institutional growth and prominence.

The current discussion of an "amicable separation" over human sexuality is but the latest evidence of a market-formed denomination unable to embody the oneness wrought in Jesus Christ. Again, the underlying questions remain:

- Where are the margins?
- Who is at the center of the church's life and mission?
- Who is on the margins?

The denominational legislative bodies in the United States are primarily dominated by the economically privileged and socially prominent, heterosexual white people. Modes of operation and decision-making reflect secular practices of business and governmental bodies controlled by economics more than by theology and spiritual disciplines. Absent from the discussion and on the periphery of considerations are those at the center of God's presence and mission: "the orphans, widows, and sojourners" and those Jesus called "the least of these," the poor, imprisoned, the sick, the outcasts, the vulnerable, the powerless.

Called to Shift the Margins

John Swinton, a Scottish theologian at The University of Aberdeen, writes and speaks extensively on theology and disabilities. He helpfully argues that Jesus did not *go to* the margins as much as he *shifted* the margins. Those on the margins of society became the center of Jesus's presence and ministry, while the religiously, socially, and economically prominent were on the margins of his presence and ministry.[6] Wesley

---

[5] See C. C. Goen, *Broken Churches, Broken Nation: Denominational Schisms and the Coming of the Civil War*, Mercer University Press, 1997, first published in 1985. See especially the chapter entitled "A Failure of Leadership," which documents the tragic consequences of the MEC church's dividing over slavery in 1844 and the reasons for the church's failure, including the idolatry of church growth.

[6] John Swinton, "Doing Small Things With Extraordinary Love: Congregational Care of People Experiencing Mental Health Problems," ABC Religion and Ethics (website) accessed October 29, 2020, https://www.abc.net.au/religion/

> *Now is the time for the heirs of Wesley who claim ultimate loyalty to Jesus to intentionally shift the margins of the denomination's life and ministry with the vulnerable, the weak, the poor, the outcasts, the pushed-aside at the center.*

followed Jesus's example in 18th-century England. The sophisticated, well-educated, academically gifted, and religiously privileged Anglican priest intentionally and effectively shifted the margins of his own circle of friendships and ministry to those on the margins. He developed strategies and practices in relation to those who lived in poverty, for children, the imprisoned, the sick, and those outside the established church's participation.

Now is the time for the heirs of Wesley who claim ultimate loyalty to Jesus to intentionally shift the margins of the denomination's life and ministry with the vulnerable, the weak, the poor, the outcasts, the pushed-aside at the center. It is the call of the gospel! If the leaders of 19th- and 20th-century American Methodism could intentionally and effectively turn the denomination toward the more economically, socially, and politically privileged and prominent, we who are now among the privileged and powerful can shift toward those on the margins of both the church and society.

The call is inherent in the official UMC mission statement first adopted by the General Conference in 2000: "to make disciples of Jesus Christ." The prominent rationale for the adoption of the mission statement was the reversal of the membership decline over the last half-century. The market logic and evangelism-as-church-growth dominated the arguments.

At the Council of Bishops meeting in the fall of 2004, the decision was made to move away from the Initiative on Children and Poverty and focus on implementing the mission statement. Again, much of the discussion focused on the necessity of reversing the decline in membership and attendance. Bishops actively involved in the Children's

doing-small-things-with-extraordinary-love-congregational-care-o/10098938.
An excellent treatment of the implications of Swinton's perspective on forming communities of justice and compassion can be accessed here: Groundings: Finding Belonging in the Margins | Citizens for Public Justice (cpj.ca).

Initiative raised the question: Toward what end is the church to make disciples? "The transformation of the world" was the agreed-upon response. During the subsequent four years, bishops put the two statements together in private and public discussions: "to make disciples of Jesus Christ for the transformation of the world." The bishops presented the revised addition to the General Conference of 2008, and it was approved overwhelmingly with minimal discussion.

Tragically, the mission statement has become a slogan, a marketing phrase to sell a particular program, structure, or activity. The motivation and understanding of the statement must be revisited and transformed. It smacks of *Pelagianism* – a 5th-century Christian heresy taught by Pelagius and his followers – that elevates our agency above that of the Holy Spirit and a form of institutional triumphalism that usurps God's present and coming reign in Jesus Christ.

Shifting the margins will require that we connect Matthew 28 with Matthew 25 and the Sermon on the Mount! Relationships with "the least of these" are integral to Christian discipleship and not a voluntary add-on after becoming members of the institutional church. We are evangelized in relationships with "Jesus' bosom friends" as surely as we become agents of God's reconciling presence to others. The poor, the imprisoned, the sick, the addicted, the frail, the pushed-aside cannot be reduced to objects of our ministries. They must be friends, colleagues, and full participants in every congregation's life and ministry. Rather than being hidden or on the edge, they must be at the center of congregational life. All must be welcomed at the center of the church's life and leadership.

Shifting the margins with "the least of these" at the center is an adaptive challenge, requiring at least a generation. The shift begins within our congregations and local communities by discovering those hidden from our view. They are across the tracks from our subdivisions, locked away in local jails and prisons, confined in the local nursing homes and memory-care facilities, listed among the "homebound," and languishing in the local shelters. They may be eating in our soup kitchens, visiting our food pantries and used-clothing outlets, or attending AA meetings in our fellowship halls. They are the immigrants, the working poor, the differently abled. They are our LGBTQ+ neighbors, family members, and co-workers. Some are our family members and neighbors who live with mental illness, emotional distress, and crippling, unresolved guilt and grief. Many speak different languages, have different skin colors, and worship in different styles. But they share with us an identity as beloved children of God made in the divine image and redeemed in Jesus Christ. Honoring that identity and receiving their gifts will transform the church and the world.

Conclusion

The United Methodist Church as an institution confronts history-changing decisions. At issue is this question: Who will be at the center of the denomination's life and mission? Methodism was birthed among those on the margins of eighteenth-century British society as John Wesley intentionally made them the center of his relationships and ministry. He sensed before his death that increased prosperity and disengagement from the poor threatened the future of the movement by diminishing reliance on God's transforming grace. Wesley's fears were validated in the American context as his heirs in the nineteenth and twentieth centuries wedded the gospel with American individualism and the market logic of consumerism, social respectability, and upward mobility.

While the presenting issue before the leaders of The United Methodist Church is whether to divide into two or more denominations, the struggle goes deeper than institutional structures. The crucial theological, ecclesiological, and missional decision is whether we will be faithful to the God made known in the Exodus and supremely in Jesus the Christ. The Bible is clear: God chooses the powerless, the weak, the outcast, and the despised to be agents of the transformation in the world.

God came among us as one on the margins. He was birthed by an unmarried peasant teenager amid the homeless. He spent his first two years as an immigrant, grew up in a working-class family in an obscure village, labored with his hands. He announced the dawning of God's new world where good news is brought to the poor, captives are released, sight is restored to the blind, the oppressed are set free, and

Jubilee justice is proclaimed (Luke 4:18-19). He so closely identified with the poor, the imprisoned, the sick, and the pushed aside that what is done to them is done to him (Matthew 25:31-46). He was convicted as a felon, executed as a common criminal, and buried in a borrowed grave.

But we know the rest of the story! God raised him from the dead, thereby declaring that all human-made boundaries have been shattered. God in Christ has forever shifted the margins and claimed ALL as within the circle of God's beloved, redeemed community. At the center of that beloved community are those currently on the margins of American society and The United Methodist Church. It's time to follow Jesus and shift those margins! The future belongs to God's beloved community!

Bishop Kenneth L. Carder retired as an active bishop in 2004 after serving the Nashville Area (1992-2000) and the Mississippi Area (2004). Prior to his election to the episcopacy, he served local churches in the Holston Conference, including Concord in Farragut, TN, First Church Oak Ridge, and Church Street in Knoxville.

As an active bishop he authored the Foundation Document for the Initiative on Children and Poverty, chaired the committee that developed "A Wesleyan Vision for Theological Education and Leadership for the 21st Century," and delivered the Episcopal Address at the 2004 General Conference.

He is the author of six books including his most recent, *Ministry with the Forgotten: Dementia through a Spiritual Lens.* He was the caregiver for his wife of 59 years, Linda, until her death from dementia in October 2019.

CHAPTER SEVEN
Leadership Investment for a Vital Future

Rodney Smothers

Leadership that is vision-filled, risk-taking and innovative is essential to the future of the United Methodist Church. Our obsession with rearranging the chairs on the deck of the Titanic will not serve us well moving forward. Our leadership must be developed with new tools for new tasks. While history, polity and theology have their place, the emerging generations of leaders must also be equipped with innovative systems and strategies that lead our governing bodies and congregations with new insights and opportunities based on a fast-moving cultural change that demands nimble, adaptive and flexible styles of learning and leadership.

A couple of years ago, Lia McIntosh, Jasmine Rose Smothers and I authored a book titled Blank Slate: Write Your Own Rules for a 22nd-Century Church Movement. We began the outline of that book by discussing the Old Rules based on the cultural context of Traditionalists (born 1945 or before), Boomers (born 1946-1964), and Gen-Xers (born 1965-1980). We framed the decision-making philosophies based on what was informing the mindsets of those generations.

We continued that discussion of the New Rules as framed by the decision mindsets of the millennials (born 1981-1995) and Generation Z (born 1996-2010). It soon became apparent that our churches are being governed by a generational mindset that is no longer in alignment with the changing culture and ministry mindset that is needed to lead our churches into vital and productive decision-making.

The ministry landscape has changed; society has changed; and the church as we once knew it has changed. Seven mindsets that are driving that change are:

- **Community** is formed differently. Digital and technological relationships are more pronounced and, for good or bad, now dominate how people gather, dispense information and make decisions about life and their priorities. The church is no longer just a place; it is now a movement, a conversation and a community that is informed by more than just a sermon on Sunday morning.

- **Outcomes** drive allegiance. It has been said that all politics are local; the same is now true of denomination and congregational loyalties. Religion is now viewed as one of many influences that determine people's thoughts, disciplines and behaviors. Younger churchgoers are more loyal to their local tribe than to a denominational emphasis.

- **Innovation** is mission critical. The church is only as important as it is relevant and responsive to the emerging needs of its followers. Younger people shop in several places with several different tools until they find the goods and services that meet their needs. Brand loyalty no longer drives commitment. Convenience is driving when and where these younger generations invest their time, talents, gifts, service and witness.

- **Storytelling and interactive communication** have drastically changed how people receive biblical information. Production has become as important as preaching; technology is driving viewers' choices; and being available digitally, downloadable and on-demand has become the new standard.

- **Authenticity and empathy** now drive response and investment. With so many invitations in the lives of these emerging generations, appeals for legacy special days and offerings are unable to compete with the needs that are right on our doorsteps. People now want to see how their gifts are making a difference in real-time with real people.

- **Empowerment** is more than organizing a mission team, empowerment today means impacting a school board's decisions making, shaping the politics of a nation and harnessing real power through voice and vote. Diversity is also driving increased advocacy around giving the decision-making power to people on the pews rather than a denominational interpretation of what is right in a particular community.

- **Faith that is functional** drives spiritual curiosity. People, young and old, are seeking a relationship with God. That hunger is not being sought after in committee meetings and task forces. Spiritual hunger is at an all-time high. Organizations that are preoccupied with structural reorganization without giving as much emphasis to spiritual regeneration will become obsolete as soul-saving stations. Discipleship is needed more now than ever before. The late Rev. Junius Dotson, general secretary of Discipleship Ministries was on to something as he launched the "See All The People" campaign. That campaign invited us to understand the importance of everyday ordinary discipleship as encounter and lifestyle. That campaign asked the question, "What would happen if we stopped fixing our church and started seeing all the people Christ calls us to reach?"

These issues are even more elusive in Black, Brown and other communities where health disparities, economic injustice, social inequality, and yes, inadequate or substandard congregations are struggling just to keep the doors open for ministry. This too is a leadership issue. It is also a relationship issue. The future growth of the African American Church depends on collaborative relationships. In our current cultural and congregational contexts, the politics of separation, hate, political division, racism and theological interpretations are among the demonic forces preventing us from resetting a healthy and sustained agenda for leadership development. If we are expecting anything different in the future, this is the elephant in the room; these things are not being adequately addressed. Earlier attempts to address the lack of a leadership pipeline were developed by Bishop James S. Thomas and Dr. Grant Shockley when they developed the Thomas Shockley Youth Theological Academy as a feeder program into United Methodist-related academic institutions. Not only did this program investigate the spiritual lives of these young people, However, it also provided these young people a look theologically into the future of the church. Funded through grants, when the grants stopped – and the visionaries grew older – the emphasis on training these young Black future leaders stopped.

There had also been earlier attempts through the Pembroke Institute in Chicago, the East Ohio and West Ohio Institutes. The Bishop Melvin G. Talbert Fellows program, shaped by Bishop and Dr. Marilyn Magee Talbert in partnership with Black Methodist for Church Renewal along with the Thomas Shockley Academy, produced church leaders who are successfully leading ministries today. Those intentional programmatic efforts, though limited in scope, have borne great results. They succeeded in identifying, equipping and sending young leaders into tracks for exceptional leadership development to prepare men and women for spiritual service. The challenge, once these visionary bishops and educators were no longer at the helm of these efforts, no churchwide effort to sustain these efforts ever materialized. I once heard Bishop Cornelius Lynn Henderson say, "The challenge ahead for the Black church is the failure to create a consistent pipeline of exceptional leaders, and no one seems to care." The leadership crisis in the church is not limited to people of color, but our lingering failure to address these issues will accelerate the death of vital urban churches that serve Black and Brown cultures. We have not been consistent in creating vibrant, continuous systems to develop this emerging generation of exceptional leaders. Without a vital and intentional cadre of Black and Brown people, many of our inner-city churches will fail, partially because we lack a denominational vision for inner-city ministry.

Few Annual Conferences are investing in coaching, mentoring and next-level leader training for clergy and laity to produce innovative and transformational ministries that function seven days a week, as ministry centers, collaborative partnerships, economic generators, affordable housing partnerships and literacy and learning centers. The church's failure to address gun violence and domestic violence is a failure of our will to equip and train a new generation of priests, prophets and pastors, lay intercessors and counselors to do the work of healing in our broken communities. While the denomination is preoccupied with issues of who is sleeping with whom, we are failing miserably to address the basic tenet of our Christian mission to feed the hungry, clothe the naked and set the captives free. Failure to invest in identifying, cultivating and equipping exceptional Black leaders is yet another form of racism that harms our discipleship and witness.

Dr. Joseph L. Daniels in Washington, D.C. at Emory Fellowship and Drs. Rudy and Juanita Ramus in Houston and scattered smaller legacy projects developed by local congregations have shown us the positive impact that creative, collaborative church and community projects can have upon their community. These special calls to church and community are all shaped around unique personalities and we would benefit from their vision, witness and legacies being passed on through some forms of institutional learning. Strategic learning centers like Gammon Theological Seminary at the Interdenominational Theological Center in Atlanta are excellent incubators for preparing Next Generation leaders. What will it take?

If we are to survive beyond the coming denominational divorce, it will require a retooling of our denomination at every level. I believe that there are ten hinges on which our future must swing. Call, spirituality, vision, creativity, engagement, innovation, leadership, coaching, technology and collaboration. Where do we go from here is dependent on how we hear God's call to the future? Certainly, the pandemic has caused us to rethink how the tried-and-true methods of ministry have to be adjusted to respond to the new online, on-demand, downloadable church cultures in which we find ourselves doing ministry. While in the past a gifted youth pastor might have been our dream staff associate, today a minister of technology is our preferred staff member.

Our giving in the past was shaped by our annual stewardship campaigns; today our giving is driven by effective online giving platforms that must educate, elevate and provide ease of use for funding our ministry budgets. Communication upgrades at every level in the ministry from the pulpit to the parking lot are needed to accommodate a changing constituency. Our emerging reality is being shaped by apps and sound bites, culture wars and contextual contexts that require adaptive and innovative behaviors. Master of Divinity degrees for clergy must now be supplemented with cultural and contextual training in multiple disciplines. Collaborative decision-making with laity and informed resources beyond the theological community raises this important question, "Who will do this with me?"

Our future vision is no longer shaped by the old chart of letters on the wall of our eye doctors. The future is found in the Oculus headsets that provide a glimpse into the future based on projected and emerging data. One of the added benefits of the Oculus headsets is, even if you currently wear eyeglasses, the Oculus assists you to see additional things in your midst that you never saw before. We need a vision that is not clouded by

> *We are fighting over buildings and land; the future of the church will not be in warehouses filled with people.*

what we already know but need a vision that allows us to see new and emerging opportunities.

We are fighting over buildings and land; the future of the church will not be in warehouses filled with people, rather, it will be taking the gospel message where people are digital, downloadable and available on demand. Our research and development (R&D) investments and leader training investment must increase to prepare a new generation of spiritually trained leaders to do the necessary engagement for a society that is increasingly mobile and nomadic. Perhaps we should create within the Council of Bishops a special unit that is not involved at all in rescuing the Titanic, but whose vision is fully invested in creating new starships for our long-term viability through high touch and high tech. Evangelism is wonderful, but evangelism without engagement is short-sighted. Don't get me wrong; I know that we are in the business of soul care. However, if we are not aggressively pursuing creative ways to include spiritual disciplines in the other life skills for emerging generations, then our current facilities will simply become museums filled with relics from the past.

In a world filled with innovation, we can't seem to figure out how to have a General Conference primarily because we are bound by our past, rather than risking doing some things differently. Technology and creativity are the new platforms that must inform our future if we are to still be relevant in the Twenty-Second Century. We have come a long way from the circuit rider, and there are many innovations ahead that we must pursue. The opportunities that await us will be discovered in the innovation and creativity that transform our Wesleyan foundations of classes, bands and societies into contextually relevant small groups that change thinking, change disciplines and change behaviors. Maybe a better future is not as elusive as we think. There have been several studies over the years listing the characteristics of servant leadership; valuing people, humility, listening, trust, caring, mentoring and certainly in our present context coaching. I would add that our task is more urgent, because we must add the word "spiritual," to the phrase servant leadership. Spirituality, servanthood and service are more important than ever as ingredients in our leadership culture. Beyond positional leadership, our call to mentor and coach a new generation of exceptional leaders is paramount to developing a pipeline of courageous learners and leaders who cannot only help the church to survive but who can cause the church to thrive. The writer of Ephesians puts it this way:

He handed out gifts above and below, filled heaven with his gifts, filled earth with his gifts. He handed out gifts of apostle, prophet, evangelist, and pastor-teacher to train Christ's followers in skilled servant work, working within Christ's body, the church, until we're all moving rhythmically and easily with each other, efficient and graceful in response to God's Son, fully mature adults, fully developed within and without, fully alive like Christ.

No prolonged infancies among us, please. We'll not tolerate babes in the woods, small children who are easy prey for predators. God wants us to grow up, to know the whole truth and tell it in love – like Christ in everything. We take our lead from Christ, who is the source of everything we do. He keeps us in step with each other. His very breath and blood flow through us, nourishing us so that we will grow up healthy in God, robust in love.

Ephesians 4:11-16 (MSG)

Leadership roles in growing and vital churches now require a trained and committed laity who can serve as committed partners in developing and growing churches. Persons who have been involved in new church development have long witnessed the effectiveness of church planters who have not been ordained clergy but specifically trained in church planting that brought to their role life experience, people skills, team cultivation gifts and the willingness to serve alongside clergy to lead men and women into discipleship functions in the life of the church. Unfortunately, there has been some undervaluing of laity stemming from credentialing issues that have not served us well.

Our forward-looking leadership systems must include reinvestment of team ministry that recaptures the importance of lay and clergy teams as our new norms in growing and leading ministries that are multilayered and multi-disciplined. What I am advocating here is more than just volunteer roles. A radical reordering of the ministry of the laity as equal partners at every level of our church is essential. This radical approach would redesign clergy-only systems so that laity would sit alongside clergy as equal partners in discernment and decision making. Gift based leadership role assignments would as a different set of questions.

Does this person's spiritual gift compliment the leadership team in such a way that we have the right people serving in the right roles in the right places? I have served on Boards of Ministry where we have asked candidates about their memory of history, polity, structure and tradition, but failed to assist the candidates to clarify their call to spiritual service. Perhaps our philosophy of creating generalists for service "anywhere," has blurred our vision to seek more intentionality in searching for apostles, prophets, evangelists and pastor-teachers to train Christ's followers in skilled servant work. (Ephesians 4: 11-12, The Message).

Discernment, personality, skills and psychological testing are important. The addition of spiritual gifts, calling and anointing would provide a more strategic assessment of team-based leadership that asks the question, do we have the right team of people for the right task? Driving this point home – our future leadership investment should pivot to a team-based approach that values assessments, mission-focused, Holy Spirit-driven discernment as we staff for effective ministry and mission. How would that look? Every urban ministry team would include collaborative partners who are trained in urban development, diverse, multi-cultural, multi-contextual and where appropriate multi-lingual leaders. These are not new approaches. Over the years, several programs have attempted to piecemeal these efforts through grants, subsidies and special emphasis. We've programmed and workshopped the attempts to place small bandages on these issues, but we have not committed to a fresh approach, a risk-taking approach, that invites true engagement for the present and future needs.

I am reminded of my first full-time pastoral appointment when my new district superintendent stood with me in a massive abandoned, formerly white congregation sanctuary, and handed me the keys to the door. I said to him with my knees shaking, "You expect for me to fill this place?"

He said, "Yes." Then what he said next stunned me. "Now, Rodney,

I don't know much about growing Black churches, but if you have any questions, call me."

I thought to myself, "You just told me you don't know anything about growing a church in this culture and context, why would I call you?" Fortunately, I found some folks who did know something about the culture and context, and with the leading of the Holy Spirit, that congregation grew from eighteen to more than 600 members in four years. The folks who helped make that happen were a gifted group of the laity from all walks of life. They coached me to succeed as their pastor. As I write this article, that church is celebrating forty years of faithful ministry. The ministry landscape has changed. Rev. Dr. Candace M. Lewis, now president-dean of Gammon Theological Seminary, and I co-authored a book titled *Resurgence: Navigating the Changing Ministry Landscape.*[1] This resource continues to be a helpful resource in assisting congregations to experience a resurgence. Chapter 6 in that book is titled "From Telling to Coaching Leaders." Under the old concept of telling leaders, the ministry model was to dispense information, give a plan, focus on an event. That plan tended to be inflexible and lacked a shared vision and limited the success of the plan because leaders can be limited by their lack of capacity. Coaching, on the other hand, allows plans to develop through conversations, feedback and input from the team; systems are created to get things done; there is a willingness to adapt and adjust plans with ease; then implement and execute the plans and finally this coaching concept leads to exponential growth and capacity based on shared ideas of the team. The right coach can lead ministries to resources, proven strategies and best practices. While I have certainly shared reflections from my background as an African American, I have used many of these same principles to lead both multi-cultural and predominantly white congregations where I have served as the Lead Pastor. Principles are not color specific. Good principles, combined with good practices, result in good outcomes. Hopefully, when the next edition of *What's Next? United Methodist Leaders Discuss the Future of the Church* is written, we will have made progress beyond church divisions, racial injustice, economic crisis, political posturing and pandemic interruptions. I hope that we will ask the larger question:

---

[1] Candace Lewis and Rodney Smothers, *Resurgence: Navigating the Changing Ministry Landscape,* Heritage, 2018.

Who will do this with me? My prayer is that we will pivot to new and relevant discipleship models that invite a new generation of believers to discover Jesus Christ as their Lord and Savior.

Dr. Rodney Thomas Smothers serves as the Lead coach for rTs Coaching Associates and the founder of The Smothers Group a leadership coaching and consulting team that provides strategic leadership training for individuals and ministries.

He is the co-author of *Resurgence: Navigating the Changing Ministry Landscape, Blank Slate: Write Your Own Rules for a 22nd-Century Church Movement,* and and *A Cry From The Pew: A Call to Action for The United Methodist Church..* He is the founder and director of The Smothers Group.

CHAPTER EIGHT

The Future Church Is a Business – and That's a Good Thing

Wil Cantrell

Were it not for a conversation between Ray Croc and Harry Sonneborn, you might have never heard of McDonald's. As the fledgling restaurant chain began to grow, the profit margins produced by recouping a small percentage of sales revenue remained too thin to support enough expansion to make the franchise business model sustainable.

Then Harry Sonneborn convinced Ray Croc that McDonald's Corporation wasn't in the hamburger business. The franchisees were in the hamburger business. McDonald's Corporation was in the real estate business. From this point forward, rather than allowing the franchisees to own the land, McDonald's Corporation bought the land and sold leases to franchisees for the right to build and operate a McDonald's restaurant on the land. This provided the corporation with immediate and plentiful income to fuel future expansion.

If McDonald's had remained in the hamburger business, you probably would have never eaten under the golden arches. Whether McDonald's rapid expansion benefited the dietary habits of our society can be debated. What's not up for debate is that when Ray Croc realized he was in the real estate business the history of the restaurant industry was forever changed.

The Business of the Church

Today's church often operates as if it were in the religious services business. Churches in the religious services business focus on doing church well. The future church will operate as if it is in the life transformation business. Churches in the life transformation business focus on making disciples.

In an era when the dominant culture promoted church participation, churches offered religious services, which over time transformed the lives of participants. In a day and age, when the culture views church participation as optional at best and destructive at worst, participants no longer flock to the church for religious services.

It is often said that customers don't buy products. They buy solutions. In the future church, religious services will remain the product. But the churches which thrive will focus on understanding exactly how they can use religious services to bring about the solution people seek: life transformation.

From Doing Church to Making Disciples

Moving from focusing on doing church well by providing quality religious services to focusing on making disciples requires an increased focus on meeting people where they are and understanding the process by which transformation occurs.

Whether you are trying to get fit, stop drinking, lessen your anxiety, or become a better spouse, the life transformation process has common steps:

- Decide you want to be different
- Learn about how to be different
- Experiment with different behaviors
- Join a community of people trying to be different
- Commit to helping others try to be different
- Develop a different identity

A Delivery Problem

Many times churches that focus on doing church well have the religious services needed to change lives yet lack an effective system for delivering the services to the people.

Imagine you go to the doctor with a high fever and painful rash. You have never felt this bad in your whole life. The doctor diagnoses you with a life-threatening infection that can only be cured by one particular antibiotic, which can only be given as a shot. Your life depends upon getting a shot within the next hour.

Thankfully, the doctor keeps several doses of the antibiotic at the clinic. The doctor quickly draws up the proper dose of the life-saving medication in a syringe. You breathe a sigh of relief. Your nightmare will soon be over, and you will have a story to tell your grandchildren about how going to the doctor just in time saved your life.

Then the doctor begins rummaging through the cabinet drawers and looking under every slip of paper on the counter. Her face turns red and you notice some sweat dripping from her forehead. Soon, she abruptly walks out of the room and you can hear her talking urgently with the nurses in the hallway. A moment later, tires screech in the parking lot and the doctor returns. Her face has turned white as ash and she gathers her breath to deliver the bad news: they are out of needles. Your life now depends on how quickly a nurse can drive to the nearest pharmacy and bring back a needle that will fit into the syringe.

They diagnosed the infection correctly. They have the medicine to cure it. They lack the means to deliver the medicine, and you might die because of it.

Churches who operate as if they are in the religious services business are like this clinic. They know the greatest needs of the human soul. They have the beliefs and practices which lead to healing and wholeness. They lack the capacity to connect people in need with the beliefs and practices that will heal and bless them.

From One Size Fits All to a Discipleship Pathway

For anyone to join our church, in addition to repenting of their sin and placing their faith in Jesus Christ, they must pledge to serve the church with their prayers, presence, gifts, service, and witness.

Prayers, presence, gifts, service, and witness are the religious services we offer. But we don't require them until someone is pretty far along their faith journey. Churches in the life transformation business understand that earlier stages of the faith journey require an approach to faith more targeted on the needs of the individuals. Churches in the religious services business offer prayers, presence, gifts, services, and witness equally to everyone and wonder why so many visitors decline their offer.

The first stage of life transformation is deciding you want to be different. Churches in the religious services business assume everyone who walks through the door has already decided they want to be more like Christ. Churches in the life transformation business understand most people walking through the door are more concerned about managing their daily lives than the spiritual ideal of becoming Christ-like. Many do not even know what the phrase "Christ-like" means.

Most churches understand if someone arrives hungry, they must feed him before sharing the Gospel with him. What most churches in the religious services business do not understand is that churches must also meet their emotional and relational needs before they will recognize their need for the Gospel.

Churches in the life transformation business recognize people must decide for themselves they want to change and how they want to change. They know becoming Christ-like is the last thing on the minds of many of their visitors. These visitors may want a closer marriage, become better parents, have less anxiety, overcome addiction, or develop more friendships. If the church can help them learn from the teachings of Jesus how to overcome loneliness by developing deeper friendships, grow closer to their families, discover a sense of peace, or finally find freedom from addiction, then they will want to become Christ-like. From this point forward, they will be motivated to make prayers, presence, gifts, service, and witness daily habits because they will do anything to become more like Christ, who healed them.

Churches in the life transformation business have strategies for connecting with the needs of their communities. These strategies include demographic research on commonly occurring needs of the residents who live nearby as well as personal and digital outreach systems to connect with participants and discover their needs. At a church focused on life transformation, ministries are formed around commonly occurring needs and the church exhibits an unshakable commitment to finding help for those who have unique needs not addressed by a ministry program.

Importantly, churches in the life transformation business see their work meeting participants' immediate needs as the beginning not the end of their ministry. They carefully connect the work of meeting urgent needs with helping participants come to know more about Jesus, who alone provides the healing and blessing they discover when their needs are met. These churches help visitors who come to church looking for help with finances, relationships, or mental health discover the deepest desire of their soul: to follow Christ. Then they provide them with the spiritual practices needed to grow closer to Christ and train them to help others along the discipleship pathway.

We borrowed our discipleship pathway verbiage from the Unstuck Group at our church. You might find other language that better articulates the stages of faith for your context.

Here's what we use:

Not Interested: These persons have no interest in religion. They do not attend church, nor do they consume religious content online. They have needs in their life they don't know how to meet, and it does not occur to them to look to the church for help. They need something or someone to cause them to question whether the church might be able to help and whether there might be more to life than they have yet imagined.

Spiritually Curious: Spiritually curious people have questions about faith. They consume online religious content and occasionally attend church. They wonder if faith could help them live a better life and become better people. They need Christian teaching focused on their questions and a nonjudgmental Christian friend who will help them explore their questions without rushing them along the path to find the answer.

Believers: Believers have placed their faith in Jesus Christ and look to Him for forgiveness, guidance, and salvation. Often they have been baptized and have joined a church. They may not yet be following all of the church's spiritual practices, but they have begun to realize Jesus can meet their needs. They need a community and a close connection to a Christian mentor who can help them develop spiritual practices and persevere through the inevitable challenges and conflicts that arise in a life of faith.

Disciples: Disciples find their identity in following Christ. They embrace the spiritual practices of prayers, presence, gifts/generosity, service, and witness. They see the purpose of their lives as growing closer to Christ. They need help identifying their spiritual gifts and opportunities to mentor others along the discipleship pathway.

Disciple-Makers: Disciple-makers find their purpose in helping others grow in faith. They know every time someone moves along the discipleship pathway, a life is transformed. They want nothing more than to spend their lives offering Christ to the people they meet. They also recognize the work of making disciples as the way they will continue to grow closer to Christ themselves. They need leadership opportunities, training, and a robust support system to help them navigate the joys and sorrows of a life spent in Christian ministry.

Most churches are good at moving people along the discipleship pathway from *Believer* (Step 3) to *Disciple* (Step 4). Some churches also exhibit competency moving people from *Spiritually Curious* (Step 2) to *Believer* (Step 3). Few churches consistently help people move from *Disciple* (Step 4) to *Disciple-Maker* (Step 5). And still fewer churches effectively engage *Not Interested* people (Step 1) and help them become *Spiritually Curious People* (Step 2).

Churches who effectively help people move along the entire discipleship pathway exhibit an unbreakable focus on making disciples rather than doing church well. These churches have been in the life transformation business long enough to learn the ins and outs of the business. When they encounter obstacles, rather giving up and blaming the culture for being anti-Christian as many churches in the religious services business do, life transformation churches dig in. They keep wrestling the issues to the ground until they find an opportunity to share the Gospel in places other churches only see insurmountable obstacles.

Which church would you rather be a part of: a religious services church or a life transformation church? How would you describe the state of your church? Is your church currently in the religious services business or the life transformation business?

I hope this chapter helps your church move from a religious services business model to a life transformation model. Perhaps you are already at a life transformation church. In your case, I hope this article encourages you to continue wrestling faithfully with the hardships encountered by churches that refuse to surrender to a culture that has grown indifferent to Christianity.

The following discussion questions are designed for you to share with your church's leadership team. The answers may not be easy to discern and implement. Do not worry. The answers are not supposed to come easily. Jesus did not call us to an easy business. He called us to a business for which it is worth giving our lives.

Questions for Discussion

Would you define your church as being in the religious services business or the life transformation business?

What does your church need to do to become fully committed to the life transformation business?

What do you think about the 6 steps of the life transformation process?

Name a time when your life was changed. Did your experience reflect the 6 steps of the life transformation process?

Are your church's ministries designed with the life transformation process steps in mind?

What do you think about the 5 Stages of the Discipleship Pathway?

How do the 5 Stages of the Discipleship Pathway relate to your spiritual journey?

Where does your church excel at helping people move along the Discipleship Pathway?

Where does your church struggle to help people move along the Discipleship Pathway?

What issues that your church might have previously defined as insurmountable obstacles do your church need to wrestle with until you discover the opportunity to share the Gospel these issues provide?

Wil Cantrell serves on the pastoral team at Concord United Methodist Church in Knoxville, Tennessee and is the co-author of *From Heaven to Earth: Christmas for New Believers, Old Believers and Non-Believers* and author of *ATONE: The Difference the Cross Makes* and *Unafraid and Unashamed*. He and his wife, Rebecca, cherish the joy of raising three amazing children.

CHAPTER NINE

A Labor of Love:
How We Can Belong to Each Other Again

Melanie L. Dobson

A Story of Belonging and Consensus

As the late afternoon sunlight poured through the translucent fellowship hall windows, the congregation gathered in 10 circles, each with eight blue plastic chairs. As people completed nametags and grabbed a cookie or lemonade from the welcome table, they shook hands and gave slightly awkward side hug pats. Nervous energy rippled through the room. We were assembled to discern if God was calling us to become a congregational member of the Reconciling Ministries Network in the wake of the General Conference 2019.[1]

Leaders who identified as LGBTQIA+ and had served the church for decades as Sunday school teachers, small group leaders, and on every committee possible circulated in the room. Some people chatted eagerly with anticipation. Others creased their foreheads with worry. Prior to this gathering, church members had argued on social media and beaten down the doors of the pastors with complaints, hurt, anger, and protest.

In response to the conflict the church council created a process that included two informational sessions, four discernment sessions over the course of a month, copious communication on all the church's media

---

[1] Reconciling Ministries Network is the advocacy organization for LGBTQIA+ people in the United Methodist tradition. Its mission is "to equip and mobilize United Methodists of all sexual orientations and gender identities to resist evil, injustice, and oppression in whatever forms they present themselves." https://rmnetwork.org/about/who-we-are/ Accessed Feb. 5, 2022.

platforms, and a plan for the church council to take a vote at the end of the process on affiliation with RMN.[2]

As people took their seats in the circles of chairs, I, as facilitator, welcomed them into this practice of discernment. Discernment is "the process of intentionally becoming aware of how God is present, active, and calling us as individuals and communities so that we can respond with increasingly greater faithfulness."[3] To discern together faithfully, we committed to a covenant of listening to God and each other in silence, upholding confidentiality, and refraining from cross-talk, feedback, and advice-giving. We took a couple of deep breaths together, and opened up to the abiding presence of the Holy Spirit.

We drew upon the tradition of the Quadrilateral for our discernment.[4] At the beginning of each session, I lifted up the example of the early church's discernment on the question of circumcision in Acts 15 *(Scripture)* and read short sections of John Wesley's sermon "Catholic Spirit" to remind us to "be of one heart, though we are not of one opinion" *(Tradition)*.[5] We heard a short teaching segment from a guest lecturer and listened for a word or phrase that resonated with us *(Reason)*. For the bulk of the one and a half hour long session, we shared that word or phrase in a practice called group spiritual direction, which embodies the tradition of the early Methodist class meetings and has roots in ancient Christian contemplative tradition. *(Tradition* and *Experience)*.[6]

---

[2] The four sessions each had a different outside teacher, and included the topics "Biblical Perspectives on Homosexuality" which was taught by a New Testament professor, "The Book of Discipline of the UMC and Homosexuality," which was taught by a clergyperson (not appointed to this church), "How Does Our Church live out Its Identity and Mission Statement," which was taught by a church leader, "What It Means to Be a Member of Reconciling Ministries Network," which was taught by a RMN leader. Total attendance over the four sessions was 184 people, with an average of about 45 people for each session.

[3] Elizabeth Liebert, *The Way of Discernment: Spiritual Practices for Decision-Making*, Westminster John Knox Press, 2008.

[4] Garrie Stevens, Pamela Lardear, and Sharon Duger, *Seeking & Doing God's Will: Discernment for the Community of Faith*, Discipleship Resources, 1998

[5] John Wesley, "Catholic Spirit," in *John Wesley's Sermons: An Anthology*, ed. Albert Outler and Richard Heitzenrater, Abingdon Press, 1991.

[6] The actual questions used in each of the four sessions were: 1. When the speaker was speaking, what one word or phrase captured your attention? (After a minute of silence, then the individuals in the circle shared just the word or phrase.) 2. What in your past or present life made that word or phrase speak to you? What in your life caused that word to captivate you? (Two minutes to share, with the facilitator keeping time.)3. If Jesus is sitting beside you, what would you say to Jesus about that phrase or word? What do you think Jesus would say back? (three minutes to share) After completing this time of group spiritual direction, the invitation was given for people to silently raise their hands for their choice for one of three options: "Are you comfortable, are you not comfortable, or are you unsure with our church affiliating with Reconciling Ministries Network?" Many thanks to Jim Dent, senior pastor at Greenville First Baptist Church, for inspiring our Discernment Implementation Team with their prayerful process of discernment on becoming welcoming and affirming of LGBTQIA+ people. We used a form of lectio divina combined with the structure of group spiritual direction in the form of these discernment sessions.

Group spiritual direction is a sacred circle of listening to each other with God.[7] In its renewed contemporary practice it has a clear structure of silence, sharing, open-ended responses, and prayer. Every person shares their experience of life with God and listens in turn to everyone else in the circle.[8]

As the people in the circles in that fellowship hall began to share how God might be speaking to them through a word or phrase, I saw attentive faces, heard only the voices of storytellers as others held silence and felt the deep listening in the times of silent prayer. During all four sessions the energy of the room palpably shifted from nervousness to warmth and compassion as people shared the stories of their lives with God.

At the end of each discernment session, I invited people to raise their hands if they wanted to join Reconciling Ministries Network (rmnetwork.org). The fellowship hall space filled with palms held high in affirmation of joining RMN. I clearly saw the Spirit moving us to unity and consensus out of our listening to each other with God. Afterward, people hugged and smiled together, lingering in their circles. This spirit of peace pervaded all the sessions. One participant said, "I could have stayed longer. I can't believe that I don't want to leave a church meeting on a Sunday afternoon. Instead of coming away covered in conflict, I feel connected to other people and to God."

After the discernment sessions concluded in the late summer of 2019, the church council met to decide on RMN affiliation in the church's chapel. All were welcome, and anticipation in the crowded chapel ran high. Those of us on the discernment leadership team presented the process and named the spirit of unity that developed throughout the four discernment sessions that summer. We prayed, and then members of the church council placed their vote in the offering plate. We nervously conversed and milled about in the chapel as the vote was tabulated. The vote came back and it was unanimous for joining RMN! The congregation erupted into a boisterous round of applause for several minutes, the sound rebounding off the chapel's stone walls like a joyous shout. The explosion of relief, joy, and wonder reverberated throughout us; our labor

---

[7] Patience Robbins, Shalem Friday blog post, March 3, 2017.

[8] See the end of the chapter for an outline of a practice of group spiritual direction, which includes the timing structure.

of love in the discernment sessions had clearly brought us together to consensus.

We would need to keep living into this decision as a church, but the outcome was clear. We claimed our identity as a church that welcomed and affirmed everyone. We are a place where everyone - regardless of gender, sexuality, race, class, socio-economic level, ability, or age- belongs. Coming to a consensus through group spiritual direction enabled us to move through our conflict, hold together as a community, and to continue our work of justice and hospitality. We abided with the Holy Spirit and discerned the way God was calling us to go...together.

The Gifts of Group Spiritual Direction to a Bereft and Grieving Church

We might wonder if God still abides with a church mired in centuries of racism, sexism, and colonialism. For a denomination transformed by the pandemic to have less participation and resources, this practice of group spiritual direction might help us to determine, "Are We Yet Alive?"[9] For a church facing ongoing separation and schism – and unsure if it holds the energetic or financial capacity required for division or financial capacity required for division exists – this spiritual practice out of our Wesleyan tradition can help us discern paths forward. For clergy who are exhausted, burned out, and considering leaving their ministry altogether, small circles of listening offer a means of grace. For Christians worn out by struggles to survive and adapt in an ongoing – unable to drag themselves to worship, much less to a church committee meeting – this practice provides spiritual invigoration and a touch with the Holy – in a time when God may have seemed absent. For our young people, who feel alone, isolated, depressed, and anxious, this way of being with others provides healing. If anything can bring hope, if anything can offer the possibility of seeing the image of God in each other, and if anything can mend us together, the Holy Spirit can through our participation in circles of holy listening.

To the bereft, conflicted, grieving, struggling, suffering, loss-laden,

---

[9] Penned by Charles Wesley in the 1740s, John Wesley began using this hymn in annual society meetings and conferences by the 1780s as a practice of "holy conferencing." It has become a standard to sing at annual conferences ever since. Geoffrey Moore, "History of Hymns: "And Are We Yet Alive" https://www.umcdiscipleship.org/resources/history-of-hymns-and-are-we-yet-alive. Accessed Feb. 5, 2022.

Spirit-filled, hope-possible people of the United Methodist Church – group spiritual direction offers six gifts of belonging[10]:

- Belonging honors the Wesleyan tradition of group spiritual direction in class meetings.

- Belonging revives the means of grace found in "holy conferencing."

- Belonging welcomes smallness.

- Belonging brings healing.

- Belonging cultivates unity.

- Belonging leads to consensus.

Taken together, these gifts of belonging, as revealed through group spiritual direction, can work a miracle – a miracle that sounds like applause reverberating for several jubilant minutes off stone walls. The miracle of Pentecost, when God made one body out of disparate peoples who couldn't hear each other, who didn't speak the same language and didn't agree about theology – can still catch flame in our midst. I'll unpack each of these gifts as a hopeful offering to a church in desperate need of learning how to belong to each other again and of discerning a graceful way forward.

The First Gift: Belonging honors the Wesleyan tradition of group spiritual direction in class meetings

Those circles of chairs in my church's fellowship hall resemble prior sacred circles in our story as Methodists. In the mid-1700s in England, people sat in circles on couches, chairs, settees, benches, school desks – whatever was available. These circles of small groups, called "class meetings," would meet "in homes, shops, school rooms, attics – even coal bins – wherever there was room for ten or twelve people to assemble."[11]

---

[10] Many thanks to Rev. Dr. Willie James Jennings for articulating the healing power of belonging to overcome the divisional power of White supremacy. Willie James Jennings, *After Whiteness: An Education in Belonging, Eerdmans*, 2020.

[11] David Michael Henderson, "John Wesley's Instructional Groups," Ann Arbor, Michigan: University Microfilms International, UMI 8029228 as quoted in Tracy, 120 in *Spiritual Direction and the Care of Souls*, ed. Gary Moon and David Benner, IVP Academic, 2004.

As they gathered, these earliest Methodists met neighbors with whom they might not share much commonality on the surface. People of different ages, socio-economic levels, genders and sexualities, marital statuses, and hometowns joined in one class meeting. A first-time participant might have felt anxious and uncomfortable in this unusual gathering of difference.

In this diverse circle, a class leader stood up and welcomed everyone. She led them in robust singing and then offered some guidelines for their time together – to do no harm, to do good, and to practice life with God together.[12] The leader shared vulnerably about her own life with God – where she had fallen short or where she had experienced God in scripture or prayer. Looking at the gathered circle, she then asked each person to share concerning the question of "how their souls prosper?"[13] In turn, each person offered their deepest joys, disappointments, and struggles from their week and received holy listening and encouragement from the others.[14]

John Wesley enthusiastically endorsed class meetings, as he wrote:

> *It can scarce be conceived what advantages have been reaped from this little prudential regulation [the class meetings]. Many now happily experienced that Christian fellowship of which they had not so much as an idea before. They began to "bear one another's burdens" and "naturally" to "care for each other. . . advice or reproof was given as need required, quarrels made up, misunderstandings removed. And after an hour or two spent in this labour of love, they concluded with prayer and thanksgiving.[15]*

This "labour of love" was truly the gift of group spiritual direction, through which early Methodists discerned how to belong together with God across and through all their differences and diversity. In a world that was rapidly industrializing and in which people experienced the loss of family, kin, and home villages as they moved to cities, they heard each

---

[12] Kevin Watson, *The Class Meeting: Reclaiming a Forgotten (and Essential) Small Group Experience*, Seedbed, 2014. These are the General Rules, established by John Wesley to order the class meetings. Jones, 86-87 notes that the following of the General Rules in the class meetings was not unlike a monastic "chapter of faults" in which monks meet weekly for feedback around how well they are living the monastic rule.

[13] John Wesley, "General Rules," in *Works of John Wesley, Bicentennial Edition*, Abingdon, 1989.

[14] W. Paul Jones, *The Art of Spiritual Direction: Giving and Receiving Spiritual Guidance*, Upper Room Books, 2002.

[15] Wesley, "A Plain Account of the People called Methodists," in *Works*, 9:262.

other's sacred stories and experienced communion. They kept coming back for that belonging and grew a movement.[16] Indeed, the Wesleyan movement "discloses [communal] spiritual direction as a central reason for the [Methodist] church's existence."[17]

With the growth of the Sunday school movement in the 1800s and the development of program-based churches, class meetings and their habit of group spiritual direction declined. Yet, the practice of listening for God at work in the text of our lives can enable us to reclaim a gift of Methodism that can help us to belong to each other again. It just takes pulling up a few chairs with a good leader, some general rules, and the process of silence and listening in group spiritual direction, then asking, "how is it with your soul?"[18]

The Second Gift: Belonging revives the means of grace found in holy conferencing

John Wesley defined a means of grace as "outward signs, words, or actions, ordained of God, and appointed for this end, to be the ordinary channels whereby [God] might convey to [all], preventing, justifying, or sanctifying grace."[19] Wesley recognized five instituted – given by Christ – means of grace: prayer, reading scripture, sacraments, fasting, and Christian conferencing. Christian conferencing, which is the gathering of Christians for mutual guidance, describes group spiritual direction.[20] Early Methodist polity, such as societies, class meetings, and bands,

---

[16] Watson, 22. "A strong case can be made that the class meeting was the single most important factor to the growth of early Methodism and to the retention of converts within Methodism."

[17] Jones, *The Art of Spiritual Direction*. He also notes how Wesley's development of a rule of life (General Rules) and canon law (the documents such as the *Explanatory Notes on the New Testament* and *Large Minutes* that would eventually form the *Book of Discipline*) resembled a monastery's use of a regla, or Rule.

[18] Priscilla Pope-Levinson, *Models of Evangelism*, Baker Academic, 2020. Scott Kisker has updated the question to "how is your life with God?" which is an excellent question of spiritual direction. Kevin Watson in his book *The Class Meeting: Reclaiming a Forgotten and Essential Small Group Experience* also reclaims the class meeting as a historic practice for small group community. What I've done is to pair the tradition of the class meeting with the structure and process of group spiritual direction, which ensures everyone's voice is heard in complete mutuality and that silence is used for discernment and intercessory prayer. Group spiritual direction gives a clear process for how to answer "how is it with my soul" in a way that builds community – and helps people answer a sometimes intimidating question.

[19] John Wesley, *The Works of John Wesley*, Zondervan Publishing House.

[20] Tracy, "Spiritual Direction in the Wesleyan-Holiness Tradition," IVP Academic, 2004. Tracy notes that Wesley didn't use the term "direction" because it put too much power in the hands of the spiritual guide. It could also be that it had too many Catholic connections and he would have run the risk of being accused of "popery." However, Christian conferencing as Wesley understood it is undeniably the older and more ancient form of Christian discernment in community known as group spiritual direction.

all represented forms of Christian conferencing – and especially the community formation developed in class meetings.[21]

What a loss that our contemporary Methodist gatherings – whether annual conferences, General Conference, or a local church's charge conference – have become a source of dread and conflict rather than of God's grace. The parliamentary structure of Robert Rules, which Army officer Henry Martin Robert originally designed to standardize decision making, has replaced prayer and practices of discernment.[22] Our gatherings focus on making decisions instead of perceiving God's grace and direction. Holy conferencing as a means of grace rarely occurs anymore in our Methodist connection.

Group spiritual direction provides a practice of holy conferencing yet again. In these circles of listening, conflict-worn clergy and laity alike can receive the grace they most need for their journey together. I led a monthly group spiritual direction over Zoom for United Methodist clergywomen during the pandemic. As their faces came into the Zoom squares during one gathering, I could feel their weariness and exhaustion. After lighting a candle and offering a prayer, we settled into silence to listen to God. The first clergywoman, named Anna, shared her tremendous weight of grief.[23] In just two weeks, she had done four graveside services, all while innovating during COVID-19 challenges. Anna also cared for a husband with dementia and mourned the recent loss of a beloved cousin. We held her in silent prayer until another clergywoman shared that she saw God sitting with Anna in the dirt of the graveside. This image of accompaniment filled Anna with God's presence as she grieved. "My heart is still sore weary," she said, "but I am remembering that God is with me and that for now is grace a plenty." Gathering with fellow clergy as a means of grace not only roots us in the Wesleyan theological tradition – but also reminds us that God hasn't left our gatherings or us. When we listen together to God, we practice holy conferencing and experience belonging through this means of grace.

---

[21] Jones, *The Art of Spiritual Direction*.

[22] Danny E. Morris and Charles M. Olsen, *Discerning God's Will Together: A Spiritual Practice for the Church*, Alban Institute, 2012.

[23] Names changed to preserve confidentiality.

The Third Gift: Belonging welcomes smallness

We started small. Three adolescent college kids, John and his brother Charles Wesley and their friend William Morgan, decided in 1729 to hang out and try some spiritual practices of prayer and scripture reading in their dorm room. Quite a small and inauspicious beginning! Morgan encouraged the brothers to visit convicted felons in the Castle prison and care for children from low-income families in Oxford. Other students found their "do-gooding" suspect and derisively called them "the Holy Club," among other epithets. Undeterred by teasing, the trio continued their small group as they practiced "holiness of heart and life."[24] These small group gatherings in Oxford University dorms seemed insignificant. Yet, the experience of belonging and social justice work transformed them and formed the backbone of leadership in the Methodist movement.

Methodism in America started small as well. In the mid-1760s Barbara Heck and her cousin Philip Embury started a class meeting in New York while Robert and Elizabeth Strawbridge started a meeting in Frederick County, Maryland. These gatherings included people of different racial, socio-economic, and gender identities and created a unique space of belonging.[25] Justice work happened as people cared emotionally, spiritually, and economically for each other across cultural and racial divides.

As Methodists, we've been at our most faithful and just when we've practiced a form of small group polity that integrates all of God's diversity and extends that care out into the world – as was practiced by the earliest Methodists in class meetings. As Methodism grew in numbers and in status, particularly in the US context, it capitulated to the forces of "White supremacist heteropatriarchy and racial capitalism…for dominance and power."[26] Perhaps we are invited to become again a small "holy club" – a band of disciples offering love and

---

[24] Richard Heitzenrater, *Wesley and the People Called Methodists, 2nd edition*. Quote on p. 47 was commonly used in Anglican small groups such as the Society for the Promotion of Knowledge, which the Wesleys would have experienced from their parents SPCK group in Epworth.

[25] Kenneth Rowe, Russell Richey, and Jean Miller Schmidt, *The Methodist Experience in America, vol. 1*, Abingdon Press, 2010. Betty, an African American, participated in the class meeting in New York. There is also documentation of African American participation and leadership in the class meetings in Maryland.

[26] Rudy Rasmus, "I'm (Really) Black. I'm (Amazingly) Christian. I'm Methodist (For Now)" in *I'm Black, I'm Christian, I'm Methodist ed.* Rudy Rasmus, Abingdon Press, 2020. I'm grateful to Rasmus for stating this sinful complicity so clearly and succinctly.

care to each other and practicing "vital piety" that radiates out into the world in acts of mercy and justice.

The Fourth Gift: Belonging brings healing

In a world roiled by a viral pandemic that requires isolation for safety and compounded by a culture of rampant individualism, cutthroat capitalism, destructive racism (along with all the other -isms), and transitory lives, people feel increasingly alone and disconnected.[27] Social science research shows skyrocketing rates of depression, anxiety, and suicidality resulting from this pervasive sense of isolation; half of young and young adults report that they feel anxious or depressed.[28]

The healing antidote for the profound degree of loneliness that people feel isn't primarily drugs; it's community.[29] Of course, Jesus demonstrated this throughout his teachings. Repeatedly (see Mark 5:34, Matthew 9:22, Luke 7:50, 8: 48) Jesus said to one whom he healed, "Go, your faith has made you well," and restored the person in mind, body, and spirit to their community. Belonging makes us well together, and so many people yearn for this communal healing.

The United Methodist Church, mired in institutionalism and over-programming, has failed to provide spaces of authentic healing community, despite the practice of Jesus and the early Christians. The church of the now and the future is no longer one of voluntary association with lots of programs and committees but one of trusting relationships and belonging.[30] Group spiritual direction and other small group practices like it offer a circle of trust in which people can experience the kind of profound welcome and belonging for which their soul longs. This gathering represents a "micro-community" that provides a space of connection, healing, and difference-making.[31]

---

[27] This is the argument of two recent books. Johann Hari, *Lost Connections: Why You're Depressed and How to Find Hope*, Bloomsbury, 2019. Vivek Murthy, *Together: The Healing Power of Human Connection in a Sometimes Lonely World,* Harper Wave, 2020.

[28] "Loneliness in America: How the Pandemic has Deepened Loneliness and What We Can Do About It." https://mcc.gse.harvard.edu/reports/loneliness-in-america. *Making Caring Common Project,* Harvard University Feb. 9, 2021.

[29] The actual benefits of pharmaceutical antidepressants are really small, based upon the results of clinical trials.

[30] Dwight Zscheile, "From the Age of Association to Authenticity: What the End of the Age of Association means for the church" *Faith and Leader e-news,* Luther Seminary, August 11, 2021. Accessed Feb. 5, 2022

[31] Ted Smith, "No Longer Shall They Teach One Another: The End of Theological Education," Opening Sprunt

When facilitating group spiritual direction, I've routinely witnessed the incredible healing through belonging that develops when we share our stories of God with each other. In a recent ecumenical clergy group, one woman shared the sense of guilt she felt as she carried the weight of a church in one hand and the responsibility of mothering a family of teenagers in the other. Like Luisa's character in the movie Encanto, she held everything together by the sheer force of her strength and effort, and she was exhausted. After holding space in silence, the others offered open-ended affirmations and questions. Suddenly, the dam of her pent-up weariness broke, and relief washed over her face. "I didn't know how very much I needed this safe space, a space in which I could be vulnerable and be fully myself and feel your love through that." Healing came in release from the guilt of never doing enough as God's grace offered rest. Her peaceful countenance at the end of the "holy conference" testified to the healing power of belonging. This is what group spiritual direction offers – God's grace mediated through communion with others as we share the tender vulnerability of our life stories. It's a practice that heals us through belonging to one another and God.

The Fifth Gift: Belonging cultivates unity

Patience Robbins, an experienced leader in group spiritual direction, describes the qualities of unity that develop from the practice. Openness to each person's life experience, receptivity to others as they are without trying to fix, correct, or change them, reverence for the image of God in others, and compassion for each person's struggle, pain, and suffering join to create a profound experience of oneness with each other and with God.[32] Nan Weir, director of the Group Spiritual Direction workshops at Shalem Institute, says there is a kind of bonding formed by group spiritual direction that transcends different theological backgrounds, political affiliations, and personality types.[33]

Lecture, Union Presbyterian Seminary, May 3, 2023. Smith argues that mid-size program-based churches will continue to decline. He forecasts that smaller micro-communities, embedded where life already happens for people, may be the new organizational paradigm for churches in the 21st century.

[32] Patience Robbins, "Group Spiritual Direction: Overview" in Shalem Institute workshop on Group Spiritual Direction, October 2020.

[33] Nan Weir, "Group Spiritual Direction: Overview of Group Spiritual Direction," document for Shalem Institute's Group Spiritual Direction workshop, Feb. 2003 (revised March 2009), Unpublished.

This unity developed among the earliest Methodists as they practiced group spiritual direction in the class meetings. Wesley described the profound Oneness in Christ that he observed from class meetings:

> As they had daily a more intimate acquaintance with, so they had a more endeared affection for each other. And "speaking the truth in love, they grew up into Him in all things which is the head, even Christ; from whom the whole body, fitly joined together, and compacted by that which every joint supplied, according to the effectual working in the measure of every part, increased unto the edifying itself in love." [34]

Through the practice of contemplative dialogue and listening to the state of each other's souls, early Methodists with very different socio-economic and educational statuses became the unified body of Christ.

In our current state of impasse over human sexuality, being the body of Christ feels disjointed at best and impossible at worst. Experiencing "endeared affection" for our fellow Methodists through group spiritual direction seems like a pipe dream.[35] Perhaps we are way too far gone from each other. Yet, if anything can enable us to feel compassion for each other, and if anything can enable us to discern the way forward, it is a practice like group spiritual direction, because it is the power of God doing the work of knitting us together as the body of Christ.

The Sixth Gift: Belonging leads to consensus

From the experience of belonging in community and the unity that develops, people can make significant decisions based in consensus. Rather than voting, which clearly demarcates "winners" and "losers," and often leaves more conflict in its wake (as happened after the General Conference 2019 vote), consensus represents a decision that everyone supports. Consensus indicates group solidarity in heart, mind, and soul around a decision or issue.[36] It involves "discerning what the Spirit is about in our life."[37] Consensus is reached when every person can honestly

---

[34] John Wesley, "A Plain Account of the People Called Methodists" in Works, 9:262.

[35] People who are LGBTQIA+ and people who experience oppression because of their identity might rightly need to draw boundaries to prevent further harm and hurt from others. Being the body of Christ should always lead to healing and wholeness for all Christians.

[36] Susan Beaumont, *How to Lead When You Don't Know Where You are Going: Leading in a Liminal Season* Rowman and Littlefield, 2019.

[37] W. Paul Jones, *The Art of Spiritual Direction: Giving and Receiving Spiritual Guidance*, Upper Room, 2002.

say, "I believe this is the best decision we can arrive at for the church at this time, and I will support its implementation."[38]

Communal consensus-based discernment has a long history in the Christian story. Christian monasteries used communal spiritual direction in consensus practices in their regular chapter meetings.[39] In the 16th century, Ignatius of Loyola's Society of Friends (Jesuits) practiced a form of communal discernment known as "the Deliberation" to come to a consensus about becoming a new order.[40] Among Protestants, Quakers developed a contemplative practice of discernment, in which they come to "a sense of the meeting" without any majority/minority positions, arguments, or votes.[41] If a Friend (another name for a Quaker) doesn't feel at ease with a proposal, the Friend's reasons will be seriously considered, and the process of discernment repeated until there is consensus.[42]

In the first conference called by John Wesley in 1744, clergy and lay preachers discerned around the questions of "what to teach; how to teach; and what to do" in shaping the emerging Methodist movement. Wesley had drawn up the agenda and questions for discussion, but everyone was invited to speak freely in a discussion. There were no votes taken; the goal was to arrive at a consensus that everyone could follow "without wounding their consciences."[43] In subsequent quarterly and annual conferences, John Wesley developed an emphasis on finding irenic (peaceful) decisions and spiritual fruit.[44]

Belonging led to consensus for the church discernment process about affiliation with Reconciling Ministries Network in the aftermath of General Conference 2019. Even though the church council did conclude the process

---

[38] Larry Dressler, *Consensus through Conversation: How to Achieve High Commitment Decisions*, Berrett Koehler, 2006.

[39] *The Rule of Saint Benedict*, edited by Timothy Fry, Vintage Books, 1998. The younger brothers had equal say to the more experienced brothers. While the abbot (leader) of the monastery made the final decision, it was one communally discerned, and therefore supported by everyone.

[40] Dominic Maruca, Johannes Codurius, and Petrus Faber, *The Deliberation of Our First Fathers: Woodstock Letters* (July 1966) Jersey City, NJ: Program to Adapt the Spiritual Exercises), 1966. Post Vatican 2 times have seen a revival of the practice of "Deliberation" in order to make consensus-based decisions.

[41] George Selleck, *Principles of the Quaker Business Meeting*, Friends United Press, 1977.

[42] Morris and Olsen, *Discerning God's Will Together*.

[43] Heitzenrater, *Wesley and the People called Methodists.*

[44] Heitzenrater, *Wesley and the People called Methodists.* Heitzenrater cites Wesley's reading of Edward Stillingfleet's *Irenicum*, which argues that the focus should not be on decisions of church polity but on spiritual fruit.

with a vote, the unanimity from the vote demonstrated group solidarity. One council member said, "Even if I wasn't personally comfortable with affiliating with RMN, I could not deny the consensus of the church and the integrity of the process. I put my full support behind it." Group spiritual direction as a practice of discernment toward consensus is a gift that Methodist churches can reclaim in a time of conflict.

Conclusion

This model of group spiritual direction provides contemporary Wesleyans with the gifts of a revived class meeting, a means of grace, smallness, healing, unity, and consensus. As group spiritual direction helped the earliest Methodists to "labor in love" and grow into the body of Christ, so it might help us belong to one another in and through our differences. Our gatherings for discernment and decision-making could become true "holy conferences" in which we experience God's grace moving among us. Becoming small might enable repentance for the wounds of White supremacy and result in greater faithfulness and justice work. Even more, a mission of the United Methodist Church in this 21st century could be to offer healing spaces of belonging through which people no longer feel alone, isolated, and depressed. We don't need burdensome physical plants; we simply need small sanctuaries of belonging – places into which the sunlight of empathy, care, and love shines. A circle of blue plastic chairs will work. Perhaps in these holy and small circles of group spiritual direction, Jesus might show up to the people of the United Methodist Church and say, "Go in peace. Your faith has made you well." Through the power of the Holy Spirit abiding with us, we could answer 'yes' to the question, "Are we yet alive?" The miracle of Pentecost could even ignite among us, shaped in the emblem of a flame and a cross, and unify us into the body of Christ.

A Practice of Group Spiritual Direction[45]

Holy Listening to First Presenter/Storyteller (3-5 minutes)

- The group listens prayerfully, without interruption, to the presenter.
- Group members pay attention to what they notice, appreciate, and wonder about the storytelling.

Silence to Hear God (intercessory prayer) (1-3 minutes)

- The group members listen for God's prayer for that person
- Intercessory prayer questions include:
- God, what is your prayer for this person?
- What do you want my prayer to be for this person?
- Is there anything I need to surrender to you in order to join your prayer for this person? (Do I need to release the need to fix, correct, change, or advise? Do I need to let go of my desire to tell my similar story?)
- Is there anything you would have me to offer to the presenter on your behalf?[46]

Life-Giving Responses and Questions (3 to up to 10 minutes)

- Members of the group offer questions, wonderings, noticings, and appreciations for what the presenter has shared. These sharings may be in the form of images, questions, words, or music. They may also offer what they have received as God's prayer for this person.

---

[45] Adapted from Nan Weir, "Group Spiritual Direction Group Process" unpublished handout for Shalem Institute training in *Group Spiritual Direction*, Feb. 2003, revised February 2012 and April 2020 as adapted from Rose Mary Dougherty, *Group Spiritual Direction: Community for Discernment*, Paulist Press, 1995. Another form of group spiritual direction based on a 4-4-4 minute process can be found in Diane Millis, *Re-creating a Life: Learning How to Tell Our Most Life-Giving Story*, SDI Press, 2019. Other helpful books on group spiritual direction also include: *Alice Fryling, Seeking God Together: An Introduction to Group Spiritual Direction* (Downers Grove, IL: Intervarsity Press, 2009. Rosyn Weiner, *Seeking in the Company of Others: The Wisdom of Group Spiritual Direction* (Bellevue: Spiritual Directors International, 2021). I also appreciate the pamphlet by Lois A. Lindbloom, "Prayerful Listening: Cultivating Discernment in Community" (www.ashmoreink.com, 2007).

[46] These intercessory prayer questions come directly from the handout by Nan Weir.

- Group members may use the response prompt: I noticed, I wondered, I appreciated.

Silent prayer for presenter (1 to 3 minutes)

- The group prays silently for the storyteller.
- The presenter/storyteller can rest in the silence, reflect on the offerings, or may feel moved to write down notes on what they have received.

The Rev. Melanie Dobson, Th.D, is an elder in the Western North Carolina Conference of The United Methodist Church and an Assistant Professor, Lefler and Wohltmann Chair in Methodist Studies, at Lutheran Theological Southern Seminary of Lenoir-Rhyne University in Columbia, SC.

She also directs the Spiritual Direction Certification Program at the seminary and is a certified spiritual director.

CHAPTER TEN
The Social Nature
of United Methodists!

Stephen Handy

This chapter offers a perspective that as a United Methodist, it is time to acknowledge, embrace, and offer each other and the world a synthesis of the theological concepts of social holiness and social justice. These constructs are not only Wesleyan but also biblical. Social holiness and social justice are realities that both Jesus and Wesley practiced and engaged in daily.

Tables Matter!

Christ our Lord invites to his table all who love him, who earnestly repent of their sin and seek to live in peace with one another. Therefore, let us confess our sin before God and one another. [1]

In this season of transition, the United Methodist Church is positioned to recalibrate and return to where most people spent quality time: sitting around tables being formed and then taking action. Breakfast and dinner tables, classroom and cafeteria tables, business and corporate tables, and even communion tables are places of formation, affirmation, and transformation. Policies and promises happen around tables. Christian tables are gathering places for conversation, spiritual formation, accountability, and communion so that we can become more Christ-like. Even Jesus spent more time sitting around tables than he did in the temple.

---

[1] *The United Methodist Hymnal,* The United Methodist Publishing House, 1988.

As United Methodists, part of our distinct DNA is in our baptismal ritual. Our baptismal ritual offers liturgy that speaks to not only our claim but our commitment to social holiness and social justice. For example, in the *United Methodist Hymnal,* under the Baptismal Covenant I, section 4, we are asked the questions:

> *On behalf of the whole church, I ask you: Do you renounce the spiritual forces of wickedness, reject the evil powers of this world, and repent of your sin? Do you accept the freedom and power God gives you to resist evil, injustice, and oppression in whatever forms they present themselves? Do you confess Jesus Christ as your Savior, put your whole trust in his grace, and promise to serve him as your Lord, in union with the church which Christ has opened to people of all ages, nations, and races?* [2]

And the person being baptized, or those who stand as sponsors alongside them, with the baptized community says, "I do." [3] As a community of faith, each time I/we celebrate baptism, we are recommitting to a life of social holiness and social justice as part of God's new social order which is emerging. Accountability to this baptismal way of social holiness and social justice will heighten our self-awareness of belonging to God and each other.

Jesus was a master of table fellowship and understood the necessity of gathering with people in their personal context. Tables that are diverse in race, class and gender, for starts, offer different perspectives on life, broaden our perspectives, and reduce our assumptions about each other. When we stay at these tables long enough and participate in listening, appreciating, and embracing God's diversity, then strategizing and working through mutual respect and holy conferencing becomes the norm. Our willingness and ability to come to sacred, secular, neighborhood, nonprofit, and even governmental tables and communicate, collaborate, and coordinate for the "common good of people" could determine our future as United Methodists. Expanding the table, and not restricting voices and perspectives, is essential to us striving.

---

[2] *The United Methodist Hymnal: Book of United Methodist Worship*, The United Methodist Publishing House Nashville, Tennessee, 1989.

[3] Ibid, 40.

Diversity and inclusion matter!

Several years ago, while sitting at a table during a General Commission of Religion and Race Board meeting, Rev. Dr. Lovett Weems, professor at Wesley Seminary, offered an invitational challenge to our board. His prophetic and challenging statement has been disrupting my heart ever since: "In order for the United Methodist Church to thrive, it must have more people, more young people and more diverse people." What disturbed me about Dr. Weems' statement – then and still today – is the idea that the United Methodist Church needs different perspectives on diversity, inclusion, and equity.

As we examine the church landscape, we have churches considered to be "social holiness" or "social justice" congregations often referred to as "conversative" or "liberal" congregations. One of the paradigm shifts that must occur is replacing "or" with "and" so that we can spread scriptural holiness and disrupt the forces of spiritual evil in the world as agents of social holiness and social justice.

We need a lived experience of love, grace, and hope embedded in a Christ-ethos/ethic for current and future disciple-making. Instead of getting distracted by the rhetoric and proposals that divide us, we need to hear the call to obedience from God so that we can join the Holy Spirit in continuously changing God's world. Contrary to our behavior, the United Methodist Church is not a monolithic denomination but rather a denomination with multi-cultural, multi-racial, and multi-class people and perspectives, a beautiful tapestry that is being denied. As challenging as that statement was then, I've come to believe that Dr. Weems was channeling the words of Jesus, especially in these days of racial violence and division, human sexuality, voter suppression, abject poverty, mass incarceration, gender bias, economic and environmental injustice, and political polarization. In order to emerge and move forward, we need to shift from equipping more "monocultural leaders" to developing and creating cultures of "intercultural competent leaders," who are willing to navigate through cultures experiencing times of "consistent discomfort" while remaining in the tension as Christ guides us to reimagine the beauty of God's reconciling and redemptive acts of Christ.

Social Holiness and Social Justice are integrated essential matters!

The gospel of Christ knows of no religion, but social; no holiness but social holiness. [4]

As many may know, the passage on "social holiness" occurs in the preface to Wesley's 1739 edition of *Hymns and Sacred Poems.* According to Thompson, the intention of this preface is to orient the reader for the content and use of the hymn book. Given that congregational singing is the purpose of the hymn book, social holiness in this context relates to people coming together to praise God and to build one another up through fellowship.[5] Social holiness is grounded and emerges as love, the desire and need to love others by pursuing and offering goodness to others.

Beginning with the notion of social holiness as love, Field sees in Wesley's theology a unity of inward and outward holiness. Inward holiness is the experience of God's Spirit-enabling faith and new birth and witnessing that we are loved by God as God's children. Outward holiness is the expression of love through a life characterized by justice, mercy, and truth.[6]

Social justice is more contemporary, but the activity is located in the history of American Christianity. As the slaves were imported as property to the New World, years later the freedom fighters, their mental being, and physical actions can be considered acts of social justice. Jesus steps beyond the rule of law with the woman at the well by introducing the theology of social justice. As Methodists, people of color were concentrated in an Apartheid culture and defined by a racial systemic infrastructure called the Central Jurisdiction. In 1968, after years of seeking equity, the Central Jurisdiction was abolished, the United Methodist Church was birthed, and the work of social justice was initiated. But we are still fighting the "-isms" in the world and within the denomination. The reality of sin is manifested in the epidemic distortion of relationships and the pressures that are the result.[7] Through the years, the United Methodist Church has experienced difficulty in living

---

[4] Rieger, Joerg. "No Religion But Social Religion: Liberating Wesleyan Theology." Higher Education & Ministry, 2018.

[5] *Holiness The Journal of Wesley House Cambridge,* Vol 5, no. 1, 27, www.wesley.cam.ac.uk/holiness.

[6] Walton, Roger L. "Social Holiness and Social Justice." *Holiness The Journal of Wesley House Cambridge,* Vol. 5, no. 1, 2019, 31. https:/sciendo.com/article/10.2478/holiness-2019-0002.

[7] Reiger.

with diversity and the inclusiveness of people, perspectives, and biblical interpretations.

Wesley's praxis allowed him to confront the social justice issues of his day. In the development of the Wesleyan movement, Wesley fought against poverty, exploitation of the poor, and opposed slavery while standing for prison reform, economics, and education. Wesley was deeply rooted in Christ, while he intentionally connected and immersed his being with Christ and doing for Christ among the marginalized of humanity. This allowed Wesley to engage community in a way that social holiness and social justice were integrated.

From the beginning of the Wesleyan movement, social holiness and social justice have been essential and integrated. Although this language of "social holiness" and "social justice" doesn't locate its epistemology in integration of the two, their concepts and praxis has emerged in this day and time as a viable option to a vital piety lived out in a hopeful union of humanity within God's United Methodist Church and beyond. A conceptual connection may be present, even if the words were not used in the way some have supposed Wesley to have employed them. In any case, etymological origins do not necessarily have the final word on meaning and use. Language is a fluid, evolving and dynamic process, as is theology, and new connections are often as important as ancestry.[8]

Shifting from monocultural leadership to intercultural leadership matters!

I'm proposing an integrated discipleship model that incorporates intercultural competency as a discipleship essential and integrates social holiness and social justice. Whether we desire to acknowledge this reality or not, the United Methodist Church in America is still largely segmented by race, class, and human sexuality. No longer can we split and live into ideas of separations and dissolutions for preservation. At some point, this body of Christ must resolve the disease of race and class.

This model of discipleship is guided by *i4* leadership principles, practices, and praxis and is grounded in Jesus's encounter beyond the

---

[8] Ibid, 31.

temple. Jesus spent intentional time going into the marketplace where physical and metaphorical tables existed. Jesus spent more time around tables – sacred and secular – and all were tables where broken people gathered for physical and spiritual communion with God and with others.

This process of i4 leadership emerges with a voracious sense of self while living into a progression of discipleship-making in four areas of focus. These discipleship areas include, but are not limited to, being leaders that are intercultural, invitational, incarnational, and impactful. i4 discipleship always begins with awareness, self-awareness, and the question: who am I? It's an internal adventure through your family system, personal, communal and generational trauma, socialization, how and what you were taught, exposure to and awareness of your surroundings, and ultimately the liberation of self. This leadership model involves a twelve-month cohort that is both diverse and inclusive.

Intercultural Developmental Inventory Matters!

Before moving into the i4 discipleship framework, it is recommended that leaders take the Intercultural Developmental Inventory, known as the IDI. The IDI is the premier cross-cultural assessment of intercultural competence that is used by thousands of individuals and organizations to build intercultural competence to achieve international and domestic diversity and inclusion goals and outcomes. By taking the IDI, each person better understands how they interact with different cultures. The intercultural development continuum involves a series of behavioral traits beginning with denial (misses difference), polarization (judges differences), minimization (de-emphasizes differences), acceptance (deeply comprehends differences) and adaption (bridges across differences).[9]

Intercultural Competent Leaders Matter!

Intercultural competence is the ability to communicate effectively in cross-cultural situations and to relate appropriately in a variety of

---

[9] Hammer, Mitchell R. "Why Consider Using the IDI, The Roadmap to Intercultural Competence Using the IDI," January 2019, Hammer Holdings, http://idiinventory.com.

> *Those who claim to be followers of Jesus must be willing to cross the boundaries of language, ethnicity, class, and culture to bring and to be good news.*

cultural contexts.[10] Intercultural competency is an integrated discipleship characteristic that has been overlooked. When we look at the state of our communities – the despair and disconnection as well as the hope and opportunity – it is clear that interculturally competent leaders are needed to navigate the diversity and complexity that we now face. This is particularly true for Christian leaders because intercultural competency aligns us with the heart of the Christian faith. In Matthew 28:19, when Christ directed the disciples to "Go therefore and make disciples of all nations, baptizing them in the name of the Father and of the Son and of the Holy Spirit," he gave them their first intercultural mission. This mandate continues to the present day.

Those who claim to be followers of Jesus must be willing to cross the boundaries of language, ethnicity, class, and culture to bring and to be good news. In order to do this, knowledge of difference, humility in the face of diversity, and relational skills to build bridges are essential. Not only did Christ deploy the disciples to go to unfamiliar places as agents of a loving and liberating God, but he also routinely engaged with those on the margins, boldly crossing social and cultural barriers to bring healing and hope.

Jesus is still dwelling among us, made incarnate in the bodies of those terrorized by racism, traumatized by cruel indifference, and trivialized by the interests of toxic capitalism. In the face of these realities, the work of the disciple is clear: to serve the hurting and outcast faces of Jesus living in our neighborhoods by humbly offering good news in a way that everyone experiences it as good. The journey of discipleship requires a willingness to learn how to build bridges from where we are to all the places God is sending us.

Jesus comes to the well thirsty and as an intercultural competent leader. Meaning, Jesus was formed by his community to navigate through cultural differences by acknowledging, appreciating, and

---

[10] Ibid.

embracing the Samaritan woman's diverse humanity. In John 4:7-9, as the Samaritan woman came to draw water, Jesus said to her, "Give me a drink." (His disciples had gone to the city to buy food.) The Samaritan woman said to him, "How is it that you, a Jew, ask a drink of me, a woman of Samaria?" (Jews do not share things in common with Samaritans.) Even knowing the cultural divisions, Jesus takes a risk by conversing with this woman, thus crossing over Jewish cultural rules. In order to reach people unlike us, the predominant white culture in the United Methodist Church, alongside people of color, must take seriously this call to reach others together and eliminate the systemic racial structures with the guidance and presence of the Holy Spirit.

The writer of Acts 1:8 reminds us:

> *But you will receive power when the Holy Spirit has come upon you; and you will be my witnesses in Jerusalem, and in all Judea and Samaria, and to the ends of the earth.*
>
> **Acts 1:8 (NRSV)**

Modern-day humanity has the capacity to broaden our knowledge of discipleship and to embrace intercultural competency as a discipleship essential, not simply an option. As an intercultural competent leader, Jesus is able to walk through cultural perspectives without condemnation. After the invitation to the woman at the well, we find Jesus demonstrates tremendous compassion with her. His view of people, as made in the image of God, was affirming in his conversation with this woman. Jesus was clear that the woman's physical, social, and emotional aspects of her life mattered to him and should matter to others.

Invitation to God's table matters!

John's Gospel is helpful to our expanded idea of how discipleship should be reimagined and not taught as a one-size-fits-all model. Contextualization is critical to how and what we teach about our faith in God through Jesus. From many scholars, Jesus, after traveling for an extended period of time, finds himself at a well (think about it as a table) seeking refreshment for his body. Maybe to his surprise a woman is there when typically women traveled together to secure water. Based on the Jewish cultural norms and practices of his day, Jesus isn't supposed to speak to a woman, especially not a Samaritan. We can deduce that because this Samaritan woman is alone, she is probably considered an outcast in her community, even among the women. Jesus engages in a conversation, a life-giving and transforming conversation. Jesus risks his life by conversing with "the other." She is a racial, social, emotional, and gendered "other."

Jesus's invitation was to an awkward and assuring conversation at an outside table (the well).

Even in that moment, Jesus reflects his desire to engage across lines of race, class, religion, and cultural divisions and traditions. This woman quickly realizes that Jesus is not to be feared but honored. These places of invitation are the tables that God created and continues to create. Even as United Methodists, we don't own our tables. God creates our tables and doesn't discriminate with regard to who receives the invitation. When we gather on Sundays or throughout the week, we must ask ourselves, "Who's missing, who's absent from God's table?" Could we, as United Methodists, start to reconsider inviting people to tables beyond the church that are located in our communities? What about community tables where people are discussing life issues that United Methodist Churches often refuse to discuss?

Invitations are risky because anything can be said and challenged. Transparent dialogue is what Jesus and this woman are engrossed in. Table talk is not scripted or censored. It's real and sometimes raw. It takes courage and commitment to be in conversations where we begin to discuss how we were socialized and what we've been taught and not taught.

Being incarnational in the community matters!

Jesus is the embodiment of God. However, this embodiment is incarnational as Christ remains among and in the midst of people on the margins. For Jesus, his mission was essential, whereas, in today's cultural context, the mission of Christ is often viewed as optional and certainly not as the mandate of the gospel.

Intercultural leaders are "missional anthropologists" seeking to immerse in the other's cultural languages, values, rituals, and practices with the intent of learning and then loving. Intercultural competent leaders are never trying to have others assimilate into their dominant culture but, rather, working to accommodate one's unique gifts and contributions to society.

Instead of condemning this woman for being a Samaritan, Jesus offers empathy. In this moment, Jesus reveals one great insight about his and humanity's genius: empathy is the highest form of emotional intelligence and social engagement. Empathy is seeing and understanding the needs of others and responding with compassion and wisdom. Leaders with an intercultural competency mindset are constantly self-aware, practicing "being with God" before trying to "do for God." They see empathy as a response to the tensions of race, class, culture.

By conversing with the woman at the well, Jesus offers his diversity mindset as he created the conditions for a more inclusive community where race, class, and gender intersect. Jesus's radical discipleship embodies an inclusiveness that reflects God's kingdom. Spending time with other cultures, engaging with other tribes, and sitting at the table with people who possess different cultural perspectives only enhances how we see and love God and neighbor.

Impact Matters!

Jesus's presence and words change this woman's life. While she hesitates to be all-in, it is not until she hears Jesus claim to be the Messiah, her life is impacted forever:

> The woman said to him, "I know that Messiah is coming" (who is called Christ). "When he comes, he will proclaim all things to us." Jesus said to her, "I am he, the one who is speaking to you"

John 4:25-26 (NRSV)

Engagement is where the practice of social holiness connects with social justice. Finally, her life is worth living. Impact is measured in a radical change of behavior. The intersection and lived experience of social holiness and social justice is offered through the presence and promise of God through Jesus. As United Methodists, our mission statement is "to make disciples of Jesus Christ for the transformation of the world."[11]

How does the denomination measure impact? While counting matters as a form of measurement, there must be a reevaluation of the values that we count. Indeed, the quantitative analysis has meaning, but if nothing is changing as a result of the reported numbers, why continue to require the paperwork?

In addition to counting internal numbers, like professions of faith, baptisms, and attendance, what if we started to ask different questions that direct our attention to impact? For example, if we strive to be interculturally competent, incarnational in our actions, and offer invitations to whomever God puts in our daily path, into what, then, does The United Methodist Church evolve? Social holiness and social justice can lead us to a different set of measurements.

First, church questions must shift from insider measurements to beyond the church walls into the communities where culture is being developed and where people live and have their being. Asking community or Christ-oriented questions will take courage because we have been indoctrinated to be self-directed within our institution, a practice which has taken away our ability to create cultural innovation, creativity, and risk. Listening to our communities gives us insight and perspective on how to reach out and align ourselves with other people and jointly reimagine our communities for the sake of the gospel. Innovation will help us recalibrate our current culture so we can live into a more equitable church and create a more equitable society.

Second, knowing our community helps us integrate our thinking with others about systemic structures that keep our communities from flourishing. Identifying the areas of missional engagement with people in the community creates mutual trust, and then together, we can develop a theology of mutual, compassionate collaboration. In developing joint ministries with the community, we can better determine where the actual people and financial resources go to leverage the impact of the current and future generations of disciples.

---

[11] *The Book of Discipline of The United Methodist Church 2016,* United Methodist Publishing House.

Third, resetting the measurement criteria takes a liberating perspective. No longer would we put new perspectives in old frameworks. As part of that evolutionary process, what if we added the following questions:

- How many elementary children are you mentoring in the urban core?

- As a result of your presence, are reading levels increasing based on your partnership?

- How many multi-racial leaders are leading your ministry teams?

- How many people of different races and ethnic backgrounds are represented and participating in worship?

- What is your plan for engaging people unlike the majority of your congregation?

- Beyond pulpit exchanges, how is your congregation planning a six-month immersion experience with a different racial group?

- How many small groups do you offer concerning racial reconciliation?

Conclusion

Although this is not an exhaustive engagement of social holiness and social justice, it offers ingredients for moving forward together through solidarity of heart, head, and hands. We need to develop a culture of intercultural competent disciples who are both faithful to God and fearless of the emerging culture.

Let's think of synthesis as the emergence of something new. Social solidarity is the synthesis of social holiness and social justice of our time! This idea of social solidarity means developing relationships of all varieties and not just staying with "your tribe." Where there are no relationships, there can be no social solidarity.

Let us remember the words of Wesley, "The world is our parish,"[12] as

---

12 Wesley, John and Charles, "List of Poetical Works," *The Works of the Rev. John Wesley*, ed. Thomas Jackson, 3rd ed., *Wesleyan Methodist Book Room*, 1872; repr. Peabody, MA; Hendrickson, 1986, abbr.: *Works*, Jackson, 14:321.

we are led by the Holy Spirit to appreciate and walk alongside others in order to participate in the beloved community. Reclaiming our missional edge requires staying connected and immersed in community, especially with people on the margins, where Jesus spent his life and awakened us to the necessity of being with and among "the least of these."

Even as awkward as the integration of social holiness and social justice may seem, let us put our best feet forward as we dance together to the unrelenting rhythm of radical discipleship. Let's live into a culture of grace-filled steps where social holiness and social justice become spaces for experimentation within cultures and lead us into a new social order as a means of God's grace.

What does the future of the United Methodist Church look like? More people, more young people, and more diverse people. Christ awaits us!

Rev. Stephen Handy is the lead pastor at McKendree United Methodist Church, Nashville, Tennessee. Stephen is a strong advocate of restorative justice, serving the poor and needy, and participating in life groups for spiritual formation and accountability.

While Pastor Stephen believes in Pastoral leadership, he also believes that pastors are called to be community organizers and witnesses as prophetic voices with their neighbors. Behind the mission of making disciples of Jesus Christ for the transformation of the world, there are three areas of focus at McKendree - education, healthcare and mass incarceration.

Married to Shelley Marie Handy, they have three beloved children.

CHAPTER ELEVEN
Don't Let a Good Crisis Go to Waste

Rebekah Simon-Peter

The United Methodist Church is facing a crisis of identity. Will the United Methodist denomination split into several bodies? Have we already split? What is next and who will we become?

These questions were set to be determined at General Conference 2020. As the COVID-19 pandemic unfolded in our congregations, countries, and consciousness, denominational plans were put on hold. Instead of navigating the crisis of denominational identity, we navigated the crisis of the pandemic, including the dramatic loss of life, the contagion of the virus, and the politicization of masks and vaccines. Now it's time to assess our learnings from the pandemic so we don't let a good crisis go to waste. After all, now that we have fairly successfully navigated one crisis, we can have greater confidence in our ability to navigate a second.

United Methodist churches have been deeply affected by the pandemic. Not only did congregations experience untold deaths of members and pastors from the coronavirus, without the ability to grieve in community or engage in familiar rites and rituals, but the act of congregating itself became impossible. Stay-at-home orders took effect in many places. Mask mandates added to the sense of social isolation. Public gatherings were limited to ten people. At the time we needed spiritual guidance the most, churches and other houses of worship were deemed "nonessential services." The world changed in an instant.

Pandemics Disrupt for Good

As we ask how to get our churches back on their feet and wonder the best way to move forward, it's becoming increasingly clear that there is no going back. Historically, pandemics disrupt for good. The disruption is so dramatic that people's ways of living and dying are forever altered. Along with the widespread loss of life, the very structures of society change. Coming through a pandemic is chaotic, painful, and messy. It takes a while for the "next normal" to emerge. However, pandemics promote surprising progress in the areas of medicine, economic and social structures, architecture, politics, and religion. The COVID-19 pandemic is no different.

As is the case with pandemics past, much good has emerged from the COVID-19 pandemic. Remember when public health officials speculated that there might never be a vaccine? After all, it took nearly forty years to develop an influenza vaccine and centuries to develop a smallpox vaccine.[1] Yet, within eleven months, scientists from around the globe developed, tested, and brought to market highly effective vaccines. The innovative technology they used to combat COVID-19 was first developed in the 1990s by scientists seeking an effective way to combat HIV. As this technology was already in use, it cut about four years off the testing and approval process. The genius of female scientists was at the lead.[2]

Christians can learn a great deal from the bubonic plague that ravaged Europe from the thirteenth to seventeenth centuries and how the church adapted as a result. Studying the plague allows us to anticipate and prepare for the changes this pandemic can bring.

Though pandemics have been around almost as long as farmers have tilled the soil, according to the Oxford Dictionary, the term didn't appear in any written records until 1666 when the bubonic plague once again broke out in London, killing 15 percent of its population over one summer.

The root of the word pandemic can be traced back to the Greek, *pandēmos,* which means "of or belonging to all the people." I think this definition provides a certain hopefulness. Yes, in one sense we are all victims of the virus. But, in another, we can be agents of positive

[1]   https://www.businessinsider.com/how-long-it-took-to-develop-other-vaccines-in-history-2020-7#smallpox-1.

[2]   https://www.unwomen.org/en/news/stories/2021/2/compilation-women-in-science-leading-during-the-pandemic.

change. If the pandemic belongs to us, then we have the power to shape something new out of it.

For instance, William Shakespeare lived his whole life during outbreaks of the plague. During this time, the theater was often closed. Freed from the rigors of producing and performing, Shakespeare's creativity flourished. From 1606 to 1610, when London theaters were open only nine months, Shakespeare wrote *Macbeth, Antony and Cleopatra, The Winter's Tale,* and *The Tempest.*[3]

Isaac Newton fled to the countryside for a year while the plague raged in Cambridge.[4] During this concentrated time away, known as his miracle year, he made great progress on his lifelong quest to understand "matter, place, time, and motion...the cosmic order...light, colors, vision." He lived on a farm with apple trees across the way. Watching the apples fall from the trees inspired his thinking about gravity and physics and gave him uninterrupted time to develop his theories of calculus, optics, laws of motion, and gravity.[5]

It wasn't just artists and scientists who shaped something new out of the plague. People of faith today have the same option. The church has already made major shifts, each of which highlight our resilience.

From "We've never done it that way before" to "Whatever it takes to stay together."

Before the pandemic, invoking the seven last words of the church, "We've never done it that way before," derailed many needed changes in congregational life. Uttering the seven last words of the church was a sign that tradition had again triumphed over risk.

With the rapid onset of the coronavirus and the changes it necessitated, though, congregations quickly became aware that the pre-pandemic mindset wouldn't do. To continue resisting change would mean nothing less than abandoning the church.

---

[3] https://www.newyorker.com/culture/cultural-comment/what-shakespeare-actually-wrote-about-the-plague.

[4] https://www.nationaltrust.org.uk/woolsthorpe-manor/features/year-of-wonders#:~:text=Between%20 the%20summer%20of%201665,spread%20rapidly%20throughout%20the%20country.

[5] https://www.newyorker.com/culture/cultural-comment/the-truth-about-isaac-newtons-productive-plague.

As church doors slammed shut to slow contagion, congregations adopted practices they had resisted for years. Most congregations never dreamed they would launch Facebook Lives or online worship services in a matter of days. Yet, fueled by a desire to maintain the church body, congregations adopted a new mindset, "We'll do whatever it takes to stay together." Many congregations quickly moved online to offer prayer, Bible study, worship, and fellowship.

This shift in mindset bore surprising fruit. Worship attendance grew. No longer "homebound," the frail and infirm could worship without having to brave weather, roads, or inaccessible sanctuaries. Visitors could pop in at will, fairly anonymously. The curious could try new forms of services with little risk. According to the Hartford Institute for Religion Research, which surveyed 2,074 churches from a cross-section of 38 denominations in the summer of 2021, 28 percent of congregations actually grew over the past two years. Of that percentage, 18 percent reported a startling growth of 25 percent or more. That's astonishing growth for the middle of a pandemic.

From "The church is the building" to "We are the church"

Before the pandemic, churches were almost strictly building-based. In many ways, the care and maintenance of buildings was the shadow mission of many churches. In the process of living into the new reality of shutdowns, it became apparent that churches didn't need their buildings – no matter how sacred – in order to be the church. While a familiar hymn long proclaimed, "The church is not a building, the church is not a steeple, the church is not a resting place, the church is a people," it was a relatively untried theory until March 2020.

When the doors of the church swung closed, congregations were suddenly untethered. It was both alarming and thrilling. Worship moved from building-based to relationship-based worship. Suddenly, living rooms, parks, parking lots, and cars became sanctuaries as people worshiped at home in small groups, online or outdoors. Zoom allowed for worship to be more interactive. Worship at home with mailed bulletins infused households with a sense of the holy. Pre-recorded worship videos and live broadcasts meant worship was more widely available. It also meant that for the first time, pastors and worship leaders could rest or worship with their families on Sunday mornings. Outdoor worship connected worship with the world. Instead of being solely building-based, worship became more intimate, more immediate, and more relational.

While Christians believe that out of death comes resurrection, even the most faithful would have been hard-pressed to envision the new life for congregations that arose out of the shutdowns. Worshipers and worship leaders were set loose from decades of doing things just so.

From "Wait-and-see" to "Ownership and agency"

Before the pandemic, many churches were in wait-and-see mode, as in: "Let's wait and see what General Conference decides, then we'll know what we are supposed to do." This reactive approach has had a disastrous impact on morale, ministry, and mission. As long as you are waiting for "them" to tell you what to do, or who you are, you deflect your own agency, and become a stumbling block for the Kingdom. The wait-and-see approach is also used between appointments. "Let's wait and see what the new pastor, or the new bishop, wants to do here." But wait-and-see means God can no longer move through you. Your congregation is effectively off limits for God's work. Over the years, the wait-and-see approach has squandered momentum, delayed dreams, and stalled partnerships. It has meant justice delayed, and justice denied.

Through the pandemic, many congregations shrugged off the wait-and-see mode as they dared to step into the immediacy of the moment. Whether organizing for racial justice, offering respite to front-line essential workers, or ministering to those orphaned by COVID-19, churches sprang into action to offer on-the-spot ministry to those in need. This new sense of ownership meant that church buildings quickly transformed into vaccination sites, overnight homeless shelters, and pop-up food banks.

The Next Good Crisis

COVID-19 has forever disrupted the notion that churches can't flex and adapt. Churches made good use of the current crisis by demonstrating increased adaptability, resilience, and creativity.

Dire circumstances were no match for the faith-based community as churches rose brilliantly to the occasion. They quickly moved online, distinguished between owning a building and being the church, and expanded their sense of ownership and agency. In fact, the coronavirus did for congregations what they could not do for themselves.

As we face into the next crisis, we can choose to build on the strengths we have newly developed in the current crisis. We now know we can adapt to changes – even in the worst of situations – if we choose. There's no reason that United Methodists' newfound capacities can't be used well in the next good crisis before us.

As we approach the days ahead, let us continue to be resilient and see new ways of coming together across the miles. Let us distinguish between our identity as Christians and the institutions we have built, and let us take ownership of the moment before us. The choice is ours.

Rebekah Simon-Peter is passionate about reconnecting spiritual leaders with their God-given powers to co-create miracles with the divine. Known for teaching leaders how to bring out the best in the people who frustrate them the most, her work transforms church leaders and the congregations they serve.

Rebekah is the author of *Forging a New Path: Moving the Church Forward in a Post-Pandemic World* (Market Square Publishers, 2022), *Dream Like Jesus®, The Jew Named Jesus, Green Church, Green Church Leader Guide,* and *7 Simple Steps to Green Your Church.*

CHAPTER TWELVE
What Can We Hope For Now?

M. Douglas Meeks

Pondering the future of the United Methodist Church demands coming to grips with the divorce of our denomination. Divorce has its consequences, sometimes severe and long-lasting; it normally involves grief and hope for a new future. Divorce proceedings for our denomination could have been predicted much earlier. In fact, seeds of eventual split sprouted during the first four years of the new denomination (1968-1972). The shattering breakup has been speeded up by the pandemic. Our present crises, however, have been brewing for a long time. Even if we were somehow able to work through the disaster of the 2019 General Conference, we would still be left with an uncertain future.

So, beyond divorce, we should face the reality that North American denominations as an institutional form are steadily going out of existence. Our denomination has been one of the stronger ones, so it may hang on for a period, but, on the other hand, there are clear signs that it is on its last legs. The United Methodist denomination is seriously out of step with the present and out of sorts with the Wesleyan perspective on Christian existence. You don't need to consult the charts showing the frightful decline in numbers. Just consider the overwhelming reality: We are losing our own children. Only those who see nothing of value in the denomination will be able to hold back tears as one institution or agency after another soldiers on with diminishing resources, as the mechanism for closing churches speeds up, as the selling of the denomination's imposing real estate heats up, and as general malaise in thinking through next steps of divorce trips over itself.

Why do we have denominations, and what would we have if we did not have a denomination?

Splitting up, of course, is not new in the memory of the church. Christian history is full of church conflict and division. Paul's letters to the churches he called his own clearly show that the church should expect conflict. Antagonism was there from the beginning. Much of the practical wisdom in the writings of Paul and in the words and actions of Jesus was aimed at keeping conflict in the household from bringing the house down.

In more modern times, we can trace denominations to the Thirty Years War (1618-1648) in Europe a hundred years after the Reformation. The Roman Catholic Church continued to grow because it simply accepted differing movements and orders within its expanding body. After the Peace of Westphalia, the non-Catholic denominations, however, organized communities by region, language and ethnic identity, cultural convention, and – most decisively – by political preference, usually the politics of the prince in whose territory the community existed. They were denominated (named by) the region, culture, and politics in which they existed. Competition among the denominations continued and has not ceased right up to today.

The denominational drill has been with us ever since: When our culture and politics don't agree with the main body of the denomination, we split to be among those who are like us. This has seemed natural to us. Could a church be named and organized in any other way? After all, don't "birds of a feather flock together?" This old adage became an argument at General Conference 2019 for those who wanted to take over the denomination; yes, it was actually spoken on the floor when it seemed that the name Jesus was outlawed as well as any theological discussion that would deter the business of voting. "Conference" had sunk to its lowest level; in its Wesleyan sense, "holy conferencing" disappeared.

In 1929 H. Richard Niebuhr published *The Social Sources of Denominationalism*.[1] The book appeared between two world wars at the beginning of global economic collapse and at the high-water mark of American denominationalism. Niebuhr's analysis showed that what divided the denominations was not so much doctrine (though that always plays a part, too), but more decisively, it was the cultural, economic, and

---

[1] Richard Niebuhr, *The Social Sources of Denominationalism,* The New American Library, 1957.

> *I agree with Niebuhr. The history of denominations leads to the painful conclusion: The denomination is not the Church.*

political responses of a community to class, race, and nationalism.

I agree with Niebuhr. The history of denominations leads to the painful conclusion: The denomination is not the Church. You are not saving the church by the mere act of saving the denomination. In fact, the denomination can restrain the coming into being of the church.

How have we as a denomination wanted to be named (denominated)? We accepted a name, "Methodist," that was originally a slur slung by Oxford college boys at the Wesleys and their friends for being too methodical, and we set about making "methodical" a virtue. But what's the point of being "Methodist" if you are not "Wesleyan." So, from the beginning, we accepted Mr. Wesley's teaching – but only on our terms.

In the beginning, at the founding Christmas Conference of 1784, we declared adherence to Wesley's condemnation of slavery. But soon, we reneged, saying that, after all, you could be a Methodist and a slave owner. During the great success of Francis Asbury and his associates in spreading Methodism, the courtship between church and the nation got underway. The mantra of our nation – "growth and competition secure the future"– also became the mantra of Methodists, all the while covering over the agony of slavery. Didn't the U.S. Constitution, government, and courts that we Methodists so admired make room for slavery? Next to land, slaves were the primary capital of the American economy, laying the groundwork for miraculous economic growth: steam engines, railroads, and the mass organization of labor and firms. We simply accepted what the whole Western world seemed to accept: My freedom depends on enslaving others. And we grew, as though American slavery that Wesley called the "vilest" in history did not exist.

Slavery is the ugly, unhealed wound of the United States and of the United Methodist Church. Slavery split us, and its consequences (white superiority, white nationalism, systemic racism, massive resentment) are dividing us today. The moral dispute over the marriage and ordination of homosexuals is a smokescreen hiding the debilitating wound of slavery and its consequences. The self-destructive mentality of the "Lost Cause" has spread to all regions of our society and everywhere deters efforts to create a beloved community.[2] The "sins of the fathers" are not our sins, but the ways we respond to the consequences of their sins are our sins. Despite the calls throughout the nation to suppress the history of slavery, the church may not keep quiet about it if indeed we want to heal.

So, where do we stand in relation to Wesley now? It is not helpful to point to Wesley if Wesley is not pointing to Jesus and through Jesus to the Triune God. The scholarly work of the Wesleyan Renaissance in the 20th and 21st centuries was an attempt to correct the 19th-century nostalgic, highly selective approach to Wesley. We basically took from Wesley whatever seemed to help us grow. In the process, we not only repressed Wesley's condemnation of slavery but also selected only parts of his view of redemption.

The scholarly attempt to discover what Wesley actually wrote and did proceeded under the assumption that it would revive the Methodist denominations by giving them a new identity. But we discovered that if we are not reading and conversing with Wesley at the same time we are wrestling with the reality of poverty in today's world as Wesley did in his, then we would have a relationship with Wesley that would deeply disappoint him, for we would not be focusing on the grace God gives us to love the poor, as a sign of our own redemption.

In this time of repentance, the necessary first step in recovering from life-draining divisions is confessing that we have allowed the denomination to deter the church of Jesus Christ.

Even if the church cannot be identified with a denomination, however, churches seem to require something suspiciously like a denomination: institutions, organizations, polity, systems supporting mission, and financial arrangements. As our present denomination goes under, we will have to construct something like a denomination with a radically different imagination. But here's the rub: How will we do that without something like a denomination? This moment in history requires fast footwork: Dismantling whatever is wrong in the present denomination by using whatever is right in it and creating

---

2   Heather Cox Richardson, *How the South Won the Civil War*, Oxford University Press, 2020.

new institutions with the creative energy that belongs to children. (But where are our children?)

We should not spend our time and energy on saving the denomination as it exists or returning it to "normal," however difficult it is to give up the good ole things in the denomination. Our work is to receive the church as a gift of God's grace and to build it up under the judgment and power of the Holy Spirit.

Early theologians used the metaphor of dancing *(perichoresis)* to describe the inner relationships of the trinitarian persons of God. Today, however, it is also a metaphor describing the very possibility for the church.

But where is the dancing church? Everything in the church should begin with gleeful dancing because there is no other response to the news that Jesus is resurrected, and therefore, the resurrection of the whole creation is promised by God. But where in the denomination today is the invitation to the resurrection dance which calls the church into being? I'm afraid the prevailing metaphor is more like "walking a tightrope." A few in my generation can still sort of dance, but I don't know anyone who can walk a tightrope. It's time to stop pretending we can walk a tightrope and realize that God's grace creates in us many ways to dance. It's even possible for the old and young to dance together.

We're left with God's grace and the ingenuity and energy of our children. We'd better live in God's grace and listen to our children. In a tight place, Israel and the church have done both. As to grace, the Resurrection, after all, is all we have to turn to. As to youth, David comes to mind. Among the many signs of the loss of our denominations is the absence of a means to search for and embrace our youth. Maybe the young will emerge on their own; our children have overheard the gospel and quietly yearn for its appearance in the real world. Maybe David will appear unannounced. Maybe, just maybe, the elders can offer a dash of tested wisdom. In any case, you will recognize, I'm talking of God's grace here.

The Council of Nicaea gave us the marks of the church according to which churches in every time and space should be judged as to whether they are the church or merely a shadow of the church: Is the church Apostolic, Catholic, Holy, and One? The marks are extremely complex and must be ever freshly reflected in a new time and place.

Among several crises we face as we seek to receive the church that the Triune God is seeking to create in our midst are: 1) the *Apostolic* crisis of faith in the congregation, 2) the *Catholic* crisis of mission, 3) the *Holy* crisis of the love of the poor neighbor, and 4) the *Union* crisis of governance/polity. If something like a new denominational structure that serves Christ's church should emerge, it will be because we will have set aside our denominational ministries and prayerfully attended to these marks and, especially, the ways they relate to each other. This will depend on our being overcome by the music of the resurrection dance, and finally, after all our concocted reservations, going into the dance. (We're all the reluctant, cautious, self-deserving older brother of the parable in one way or another). It will also depend, having been ensouled by the dance, on our sitting together long enough through the night *in conference* to decide what the Holy Spirit would have us do in these crises. All the while, we should sing "Kyrie Eleison."

Apostolic: The Crisis of Faith Nurtured in the Congregation

"Apostolic" is about passing on and authorizing the faith. So uncertain and fearful are we American Methodists about authority that we have lusted after a definitive "lawbook," the *Book of Discipline,* which we foolishly think will direct the life of the church in the extraordinarily complex world in which it lives. We have tried to paste together the denomination with one law after another so that the book is now too heavy for anyone to hold, much less comprehend. No constitution or set of laws remains authoritative unless they are culled and amended according to the Spirit that gave rise to them. Our uncertainty about authority has also prompted us to trust a congress that we myopically claim is the only, ultimate law-making arm of the denomination: the General Conference.

All churches are "new start" churches. Congregations and denominations simply wither on the vine as they age with too much baggage if they do not regularly inquire about their own authorization. Even the "Book" and General Conference have to be subjected to Apostolic judgment.

Helplessly gazing at the *Book of Discipline* and General Conference, we have taken our eyes off the simple fact that the church is nothing without the assembly of those who are baptized, trust in the Triune God, and who are sent in mission to the world. Nothing in the church has a reason for existence except it makes this assembly viable and faithful. To affirm this does not make Methodism into Congregationalism. It is simply to affirm what is real. It is to hope for faithful apostolic congregations among people called Methodist.

To what authority shall we answer in this time of testing? In the final analysis, this question can only be answered in the gathered congregation. Only what authors us into being can be considered *authority*. We have four realities for our apostolic appeal: The Bible, the proclaimed Word, the lived, sacramental Word, and the Word in mission.

The church cannot live without the Bible, but, as our present unhappiness shows, it can hardly live with it. To make the Bible on its own the ultimate authority is simply a way of making ourselves the ultimate authority. The Bible is authority only as it points to the Word, Jesus Christ, who in turn points to the Triune God who is "all in all" (1 Cor 15:28). The ultimate authority by which the Bible itself is judged is the love of God embodied in Jesus, attested by Israel, and confirmed by the Holy Spirit. This is what "authors" the church, what brings the church into being.

The main theme of the Bible is God's love of the world. This is the Bible's plot: God has called everything that is into being for no other reason than that God loves everything God calls into being, and God will not let anything go that God loves. We know this because of Jesus' faithfulness to the God of Israel in his resurrection, death, and life, and his dependence on the Holy Spirit. The church is a subplot. The church can be considered an urgent, perhaps necessary, subplot so long as it understands that it is called into being to serve God's redemption of the world, that is, the redemption of everything and everyone embraced by God's love.

The Bible becomes authority as it is spoken in the preached Word, lived in worship, and as it serves as criterion of whether we preached and worshiped and lived rightly. If we Methodists want to be more open to the church the Triune God wills to bring into being, we need to change our way of preaching. Our preaching is largely deficient in the gospel that Jesus himself preached: the gospel of the kingdom of God.

The New Testament Gospels are primarily about Jesus' proclamation of the reign of God's righteousness and what he said and did to demonstrate the reality of the kingdom at hand. If the kingdom has not come, the church has come into being too soon. The church exists to show the world what life in the kingdom is like. More crucially, it exists to lead those of us baptized into God's reign of righteousness in the world. The fact that we Methodists speak often of the "kingdom" but hardly ever say concretely what the kingdom is or hardly ever seek to live in it is a deadly symptom of untruthfulness that turns off our children and society.

But the Bible and preaching cannot serve the reign of God's righteousness without the sacraments. The sacraments are the written and spoken Word enfleshed in the congregation and the world. Jesus did not expect anyone to believe simply by hearing the Word. The gospel had to be demonstrated, lived out, shown forth, and touched to be believed. And this is what Jesus did. The signs interpreted the gospel, and the gospel announced the signs. Preaching and sacraments and sending in mission belong inextricably together.

Needed in this period of waiting for God's doing a new thing to revive the church that might be in some sense authentically named by "Wesley" or "Methodist" is a radical change in our theology and practice of baptism and the Eucharist. This will be very difficult because we fiercely protect our narrow views and practices of the sacraments. Often, we talk as though our distinctive practices are precisely what separate us from the other denominations. Spending our energies on guarding "infant baptism" and "open communion," we miss the biblical understanding of the sacraments and undermine the church. The result is that we falter in mission, the dimension of life in which authority is ultimately tested.

That so many of our worship services end by sending worshipers out without conviction and energy for mission is due, among other reasons, to our understanding of baptism and communion as merely rituals belonging to the denomination rather than being the presence of God's righteousness creating the church and mission. The whole of worship should be directed toward God's making possible baptismal and Eucharistic life *in the world*. Baptism is, first of all, entrance into the Triune community by which we are named – our real name. We are denominated by the living Triune God. Theologically speaking, we dwell in God before we enter the church.

Our whole life is living out our baptism before God. If we are not dwelling in the power of the Resurrection through our baptism, what power does the church have? And then, sadly missing from our theology and practice of baptism is the reality of commissioning to mission that every Christian receives in the promises believed and the promises received and the command given in baptism. We can preach until we faint, but if the hearers are not called into the world God loves to live in God's reign of righteousness, we are but "a noisy gong or a clanging cymbal," and the church becomes just a shell of what God expects.

So, the church is the place of baptismal life in two ways: 1) it is the space in which the gospel is lived so that it may be believed, and 2) it is the ground on which we (individually and collectively) are prepared for our mission in the world. To use military metaphors, the church is not the frontline where we hide ourselves in foxholes; the church is a staging ground in which we are trained for our mission in the world to which our baptism sends us. Our baptism is about what we do in the world. In the staging ground, we are authorized with hope and courage. The world is in an awful condition, but God loves the world with God's own life, and that's the source of our courage.

Baptismal life is patently impossible without the meal the Lord has given us, for in communion, we see and taste the power by which God will create a new world. The church comes to life when we ask how to shape our worship and our lives according to the new humanity that comes to life because of the real presence of the crucified and risen Jesus and the real presence of the poor, without whom Jesus does not appear.

The church is reshaped by its practical steps to extend the Resurrection Feast to all aspects of life. This may begin with making potluck suppers viable again as an extension of the Lord's Supper. The problem in our denomination is that the wealthy don't want to have to fix supper, and working people work late and are too tired to fix supper. In our common meal, we experience the world's problems of wealth and work. The potluck supper is a good place to delve into the problems of wealth and work in the light of the gospel. If there is no place in the congregation for doing this, then the pulpit, the font, and the Lord's table are robbed of their power to serve the righteousness and justice of God.

Catholic: Crisis of Conference and Connection

Living baptismally and eucharistically raises the question of our catholic identity. "Catholicity" is the question of the scope and extent to which the church's mission is responsible. The Lord's table is the place of preparation for mission to the whole world. The church should gain a new sense of its global responsibility, which is not to assume that we can globally administer churches in every region of the world but that we must join Christians globally to serve God's mission to the poor and oppressed and to nature groaning under human misuse.

We can experience our catholicity when we see that the Lord's table, the potluck table, and the family table are all intimately connected with the question of whether all human beings (and all other creatures) will find today an open table on which the "daily bread" God promises is found.

Holy: Love of the Poor Neighbor

The great contribution of Wesley to the church universal is his emphasis on *sanctifying* grace. He in no way diminished the Lutheran and Reformed emphasis on justification, but he understood justification as the beginning of Christian baptismal existence, not its end. Justification, that is, God freeing us from our slavery to our idols, makes it possible for us to stand up in holiness. Would that our whole denomination could ask simultaneously what is holiness? We would be on the way to life-giving amendment if we would say with Jesus (and Wesley) with one accord: to be holy is to "love God and your neighbor." This is sanctification. All other definitions of holiness are meant to serve God's creation of us as holy lovers of our neighbor.

But to be denominated as Wesleyan, we must stand up in the ecumenical church to say, according to the narrative of Jesus, to love God is to love our poor neighbor. In fact, all neighbors are poor. There are many ways to be poor: economically, politically, culturally, bodily, and spiritually. The ones Jesus hung out with, the ones in whose presence he received his calling from the One who sent him, are *poor in all these senses*. To be sure, we have to be transfigured to love our poor neighbor because we are trained by our society to love only our deserving, meritocratic neighbors. Let the church we work for be a holy church, a place in which we can be transfigured for the sacred life with our poor neighbors and so find our promised redemption.

One: The Crisis of Polity, Pastor, and Bishop

Ever since Francis Asbury made a congratulatory visit to George Washington, we have been inclined to model ourselves on the polity of the United States: executive, legislative, judicial. This has given us a certain gravitas until, in the present moment, we wake up to find the U.S. polity (and the democracy it was supposed to serve) in grave danger of collapsing at the same time as ours. Some Americans occasionally glimpse that the superstructure of our government does not exist simply for national defense and making the economy work fairly but for making possible "life, liberty, and the pursuit of happiness" for all its citizens. After the spilling of much blood, we have also come to realize that this is possible only when we are responsible for the needs of all human beings and nature. Our nation will be tested in the ensuing, dangerous time of amendment according to the reason for which our nation exists.

We Methodists are also living in a time of amendment. United Methodist polity is broken; the question of how to repair or reinvent our polity is urgent.

To look passionately for a transfigured church, we would need a new way of governing ourselves. Governance always raises the question of unity. All presidents, executives, pastors, bishops, professors, and parents desire oneness. If you want to go forward, you'd better be sure everyone is united. Otherwise, the only way to rule is by the threat of an iron fist.

The church has always had to be careful about using political definitions of unity. Human beings, as a rule, exert unity by domination, overpowering, gerrymandering, fraud, lies about what will make a nation or a church great. Our tendency has been to come up with what we think is the best secular way to govern and then follow it rigidly or loosely. We rigidly say, "Follow the law of the denomination or leave the connection." We loosely say, "Do as you please as long as you pay apportionments." According to the rigid polity, unconscious but unrelenting excommunication is unleashed. According to the loose polity, local customs, regional conventions, and the ethics of political movements are treated as if they should define the union. Either stance, rigid or loose, can be used to weaponize the church polity.

To ask about union of the church, we should turn, as in all matters including governance, to our understanding of God. The persons of the Trinity are distinct, with different names and functions, but they are one. But how are they one; how are they in union? The answer to this question is a decisive characteristic of God – and of the church, too. The persons of the Trinity are one in their love for each other. The Bible hardly ever speaks of God in "is" language, except in the shortest definition of God: "God is love." God is united by love. God rules by love. We know this love supremely in the crucified Jesus. Jesus commands that we be one, but that we remain different, different in our names that relate our very distinct stories and in our different gifts that give us distinct ministries.

Whatever way we decide to govern, the church will have likenesses to secular government, but for Wesley, what brings us together in comm-*union* is "faith working through love" (Gal 5:6). It is discomfiting to come up against this love when we seek to govern the church by the best ideas of political history.

Among the oldest governing institutions in the history of the church are the pastor and the bishop. In our relatively short history, we Methodists have not excelled at defining the role of pastor and bishop, and the shoddy way we have treated pastors and bishops is one result. Any new form of governing in the church will have to rethink what the pastor and the bishop actually should be.

Not just in Israel but throughout the ancient cultures, kings and emperors called themselves "shepherds," that is, pastors. A lot of ink has been spilled in recent decades over the claim that Christian pastors of the first several centuries provided the model for governance in the West.[3] From the time of Ignatius at the end of the first century, the Christian tradition, including Methodism, has been uncertain whether a pastor and bishop (they are the same order in the UMC) should be an administrator or teacher. If administrator, the pastor/bishop could be conceived on the model of an officer of governance in the Roman Empire. If teacher, the pastor/bishop could be seen according to rabbinic or scholastic models. Usually, both administrator and teacher have been desired in the person of the bishop, and in fact, almost all the theologians we remember as major until the medieval period and the rise of universities were bishops. In the

---

[3] Michel Foucault, *Security, Territory, Population.* Tr. Graham Burchell, Palgrave Mcmillan, 2007); Giogio Agamben, *The Omnibus Homo Sacer,* Stanford University Press, 2017); Dotan Leshem, *The Origins of Neoliberalism: Modeling the Economy from Jesus to Foucault,* Columbia University Press, 2016.

first Protestant confession (the Augsburg Confession of 1530), the emphasis falls on the teacher. Since Jesus is the Rabbi, the Good Shepherd, the Good Teacher, we learn from him that teaching is not simply giving information or providing the learner with merit, but, as the Latin word *e-ducatio* implies, teaching means "leading out" into the world God is seeking to redeem. So, the work of both pastor and bishop is making certain that the faith is rightly taught, preparing people for their mission work in the world, and leading them into this work. We may reduce pastor/bishop to household manager, as much of our denominational history has done, thereby keeping them on the fence on all sensitive questions. This way may seem to be a way to hold on to the people of both sides of old controversies, but in the process, we lose a whole generation.

Teaching means speaking the truth to the church and the world; administration means connecting the resources of the church to the worldly possibilities of actual good news to the poor, both human and natural. It's a good thing to be in the Wesleyan tradition because Wesley was a bishop in the valid sense, though he sought no episcopal credentials as bishop in the Anglican Church and though he angered his brother when he ended up with bishops in America. Like the great Cappadocian bishops of the 4th century, Wesley spent his life teaching his preachers and lay leaders and administrating the institutions on which the revival and mission to the poor depended.

At times, the Methodist denominations have followed suit in creating great institutions of healing and learning. Now we are grieving over the loss of our medical centers and colleges and universities. Yes, since the 4th century, the church has created institutions that it later handed on to the state or community organizations. But now we need a church that can relate to the increasing instability of institutions of healing and learning in our society. Do we have any pastors and bishops who can lead baptized lay leaders in bringing God's righteousness to bear on these spheres of life? This would cause us, for instance, to ask about the concerning state of our seminaries and divinity schools. But that is for another time.

I have argued that the church exists to serve God's redemption of the world. The church lives between God's unrealized promises of the past and the unrecognized suffering of the present. It breathes the air of possibility for serving the reign of God's righteousness. We may not allow the denomination to get in the way of the church.

Yet something like the denomination will have to be conceived and created to support the ministry of the baptized. Institutions are necessary to the church if the church is to announce and live God's justice in relation to the institutions of society. It is necessary to keep alive the tradition that bears the authority by which the church is judged and can strengthen the coming into being of a new embodiment of the church. Past forms of the church that seem alien to our situation contain new possibilities for us. We should stop asking for only what can be supported financially and ask more urgently what can be supported only by faith, hope, and love in our embodied presence to each other. Because of our faith in the Resurrection, because we know the end of the story, we can stay in hope for the church and for the life of the world even amid the threats at hand.

Dr. M. Douglas Meeks is the Cal Turner Chancellor Professor of Theology and Wesleyan Studies, Emeritus, in the Vanderbilt University Divinity School. He was formerly dean and professor of systematic theology at Wesley Theological Seminary in Washington, D.C., and before that professor of systematic theology and philosophy at Eden Theological Seminary, St. Louis. He was a Fulbright Fellow at Tübingen University in Germany1968 70. He is an ordained minister of the United Methodist Church (Memphis Annual Conference). Professor Meeks was for 25 years the co-chairperson of the Oxford Institute of Methodist Theological Studies, which is the association of Wesleyan and Methodist Scholars in all academic fields with membership from six continents.

Professor Meeks is the author or editor of 18 books, including *Origins of the Theology of Hope* and *God the Economist: The Doctrine of God and Political Economy.*

CHAPTER THIRTEEN

A Letter to the Churches of My Conference

Kim Goddard, District Superintendent

Dear Holston Conference,

I am one of the last to submit their chapter for this book because, while I know the United Methodist Church is a global institution, all I can think of is you: 853 churches in the Appalachian Mountains of East Tennessee, North Georgia, and Southwest Virginia. You are the only church I know. You introduced me to Jesus, molded my faith, honored my call to ministry, and now trust me to lead. So, what is next for us, Holston? This question keeps me up at night, and my husband will be the first to tell you few things cause me to lose sleep. But this is important, and I want to get it right. With you and me, it's personal.

In May 2019, after the called General Conference left us more deeply divided than ever, with people drawing lines and working on exit plans, I attended a gathering of several hundred at Church of the Resurrection in Leawood, Kansas, for one of the first gatherings of UMCNext. I vividly remember small-group conversations around our hopes and dreams for the United Methodist Church moving forward. As the groups reported back, the message was clear and compelling. We envision a church, free of paralyzing divisions, where we finally return to our mission of making disciples. A church that opens its doors to hurting, searching people who long to be made new. A church that extends the love of Christ to the world, to feed the hungry, clothe the naked, and care for the sick, imprisoned, and lonely.

Later, in September, I attended the Holston Conference Wesleyan Covenant Association gathering in Kingsport, Tennessee. Again, we shared equally passionate and eager visions for a church free of rancor and division, a church that makes and grows disciples of Jesus Christ and extends its ministry through outreach and mission. I walked away from those gatherings realizing that we long for the same things; we just don't seem to want them together.

In January 2020, United Methodist Communications hosted General Conference delegates in Nashville for a briefing of upcoming legislation. The presentations included, among others, proposals from UMCNext and the Wesleyan Covenant Association. The presenters gave their reports and rationale, but rather than encourage delegates to consider and support their legislation, we were asked to support the "Protocol of Reconciliation and Grace Through Separation." The protocol is legislation that, if passed, will divide the United Methodist Church into at least two separate denominations. The hope is this carefully negotiated compromise garners enough support from both traditionalists and centrists/progressives to ensure its passage.

Now, in February 2022, after nearly two years of a global pandemic and a twice-postponed General Conference that kept us apart, we eagerly await the decision of the Commission on the General Conference to tell us when we can finally come together as one to vote on a plan that makes it possible never to come together again. To me, that is devastatingly sad.

We cannot know the specific outcome of our next General Conference, whenever it meets, but it seems all but inevitable there will be a formal and approved path to divide the denomination. The question then becomes, what does this look like in Holston? Best case scenario? Churches and clergy who exit the United Methodist Church will move to a new denomination(s) poised to receive them and move them toward growth. Traditional, progressive, and centrist churches and clergy remaining in the post-separation United Methodist Church will grow as they focus again on the mission of being and making disciples. There will be resignation but no rancor in the parting, relief but no celebration. Best. Case. Scenario. But make no mistake, even this optimistic future is, at best, a second best, and we all bear the loss.

In Holston, post-separation United Methodist churches, Global Methodist churches, and progressive churches ALL lose important voices long heard and relied upon. We lose the voices on the "other side," the bold, sometimes angry, always irritating, voices of dissent that disrupt and disturb. When we are present together to listen, these voices may just push us to repentance or challenge us to change. In the past, we sometimes even called them prophets. In a post-separation church, they are voices of another tribe, so we won't hear them at all. It is, at best, a second best.

In a world already torn by anger and division, we lose the chance to speak a different narrative and become just another church fight that ended badly. Holston is not a place that does "enemies" well. For the most part, while there are well-defined disagreements, we express those differences in language that is not purposely hurtful. We disagree, and sometimes we are disagreeable, but there are few real enemies here. To walk away from each other forces us into winners and losers, us and them, and we all lose. Our corner of central Appalachia little needs another denomination, but 158,000 Holston Methodists choosing to stand and work together with "one heart, though we are not of one opinion" could make a difference. Our world needs the same from the rest of the 12.5 million of us. It is, at best, a second best.

We seem to have the idea we will be stronger, more faithful, and poised to grow if we can finally and fully part company with the element of the church with which we disagree. Maybe I could see the appeal in that argument if I only consider the United Methodist Church as an institution: an institution that is a nameless, faceless, impersonal structure I can hold at arm's length and criticize and blame when things go wrong. It's much harder to consider walking away when the United Methodist Church is Holston or your local congregation; when the institution has faces, and those faces are known; when the faces have names, and the names are colleagues and church members and Sunday school teachers and youth leaders and camp counselors and pastors and mentors and friends. Then it becomes personal … and painful. It is, at best, a second best.

For us, the splintering started taking shape after the 2019 called General Conference. Some lifelong United Methodists are leaving their local church and the denomination. They leave because we do not welcome LGBTQ+ persons into the fullness of membership and ministry in the church. They leave because we do welcome LGBTQ+ persons into the fullness of membership and ministry in the church. They leave because they are tired of arguing about it. In the end, they leave, and we all lose. A few churches removed "United Methodist" from their names and say they are now independent or nondenominational, anything but United Methodist. Some churches and clergy are members and supporters of the Wesleyan Covenant Association and plan an exit to the Global Methodist Church as soon as a path is provided. Others wait to see what a post-separation United Methodist Church will look like and may exit if a more progressive denomination forms. Either way, the plan is to leave if we disagree. It is, at best, a second best.

Maybe our current dilemma just proves we still believe in sanctification, that we are going on to perfection, but we aren't there yet. So, whenever General Conference meets, I will be there because you entrusted me with one of your representative votes. I do not take that responsibility lightly, and I will do my best to represent you well. If legislation makes it to the floor of General Conference for a vote that allows our denomination to divide, be it The Protocol or something similar, I intend to vote for its passage. I intend to vote for the path of division that offers the least amount of blaming and bitterness. I will vote for the path that allows us to hold each other loosely when we cannot hold each other close. I just don't have the stomach for making enemies and rivals of friends who disagree. Then, I will work to maintain those relationships even at a distance. We still have so much more in common than what divides us.

As much as is possible, I still believe we are stronger together, and the reason I cling to this conviction is simple: I learned it in The United Methodist Church; I learned it from you, Holston. It is the reality I have experienced over thirty-seven years of pastoral ministry. I know it because I am an ordained woman, and there were and are individuals and local churches in Holston who believe I am incompatible with Christian teaching. In 1983, my home circuit approved me as a candidate for ministry at a time they would have struggled to receive a female pastor. But they knew me and loved me, and that was enough. I was received by all but a few in my first appointment, not because the churches were excited to receive their first female clergy, because they weren't. Still, they stayed, and they let me stay. Over the next four years, we discovered we agreed far more than we disagreed, and we grew...together. This is the only church I know.

When the dust settles, I want to be part of a church that affirms the fullness of God's grace and full participation in the church to LGBTQ+ persons. I want to be part of a church that extends that same grace to those who hold traditional beliefs on marriage and sexuality. I long to be part of a church that embraces a passionate belief in the inspiration and authority of scripture and allows room for thoughtful, prayerful differences of interpretation. For these reasons, I will remain in the expression of Methodism that offers the broadest, most generous community for being and making disciples. I fervently hope and pray Holston joins me there.

So how do we live in this seemingly endless waiting time? The Word Made Flesh calls the church to proclaim the Gospel, feed the hungry, clothe the naked, reach the lost, and make disciples. This is our mission, vision, commission, and calling today and every day. It has not and will not change. We have a calling to fulfill. My prayer for us all is that we are found faithful to the task.

With gratitude and hope for the journey with you,

I am sincerely yours,

Kim

Kim Goddard currently serves as District Superintendent in the New River District of Holston Conference. She led Holston's Delegation to the called General Conference in 2019 and is first elected clergy delegate to the 2020 General Conference.

> *"My ancestry runs through generations of farmers, railroad workers and coal miners. Through their love and witness, I received the priceless gifts of grace through faith in Jesus Christ, a home in the United Methodist Church, appreciation for a good story, and a love for the mountains."*

CHAPTER FOURTEEN
What Should We Do With Our Houses of Worship?

Thomas Edward Frank

The United Methodist Church has, at most, about ten thousand viable local churches in the United States. That leaves somewhere between fifteen to twenty thousand local churches that are not and whose houses of worship stand empty all or most of the time. They have little staff or lay leadership, if any. Their programs are limited, and many rely on annual homecoming events to stay afloat. Few have funds on hand to maintain their buildings. For many, the generation that sustained their place of worship into the 21st century is passing from the scene.

Let that sink in. The United Methodist Church has thousands of virtually vacant and largely underutilized houses of worship in which the denomination has an equitable interest through the trust clause governing property – and this does not even assess the situation in Europe and elsewhere as similar issues emerge. Increasing numbers of religious buildings of all traditions are popping up on the real estate market. A quick look at real estate websites across the US reveal many of these buildings are being sold as possible private residences. The United Methodist Church has joined in that market, along with the Roman Catholics and many other traditions, and the results show up in the declining numbers of local churches each year.

Annual conferences vote on closing churches, which has long been known as a tearful moment at conference sessions as the loyal remnant pleads for their church to be kept open. Sometimes a property can be sold to that remnant to become some other kind of church, a scenario more likely in rural areas than in cities. Sometimes the bishop and cabinet choose not to appoint a preacher to a particular local church and let the clock tick down. But short of these possibilities, many buildings are turned over to the conference boards of trustees to be put on the market.

The United Methodist Church's real estate woes are not going to get better. The trend is toward growing numbers of vacancies or decaying buildings through the 2020s. Yet few annual conferences have any kind of strategy in place to systematically cope with this situation. Most handle each location piecemeal and go back to promoting their latest program for "evangelism" and membership growth. This strategy, if one can call it that, is a proven failure for most local churches.

So, if selling houses of worship one by one is not going to be effective, what is? Are there alternatives to selling? How can congregations that retain some viable leadership and resources make headway with an underutilized building that languishes under deferred maintenance year after year?

Yes, there are alternatives, but few conferences seem prepared to explore them. I have worked with Partners for Sacred Places for almost twenty years now in several capacities: as a consultant to their programs, a board member, and board chair. Partners for Sacred Places is a nonsectarian, national nonprofit that has developed a remarkable range of resources for helping congregations with older buildings. Most recently I have served as a member of the advisory board for the National Fund for Sacred Places, a cooperative venture of the Lilly Endowment Inc., the National Trust for Historic Preservation, and Partners for Sacred Places. The funds on hand are minimal compared to the national need, but the National Fund has served to bring a lot more public attention to the issue: what do we as a society and culture want to see happen with historic houses of worship, many of which are landmarks of identity and sense of place from cities to the countryside across the nation?

In working with Partners for Sacred Places, I have participated in various conversations with UM annual conferences about offering the training and consulting services Partners has available. Yet all too often – in fact, most of the time – the talk has gone nowhere. Proposals get snagged in the approval process for various reasons. Perhaps it's not a funding priority for the conference or a district superintendent doesn't trust or think an outside agency is warranted. The training programs that have been completed have largely been productive, but their impact is slight compared to the scope of need.

The United Methodist Church cannot address its property issues without some fundamental changes of perspective.

1. ***Houses of worship are a tremendous asset with unrealized potential.*** They are among the only gathering places in their communities. They have spaces to host public meetings, concerts, social services, classes, centers for children or older adults. They are buildings honored for their history, their symbolism of spiritual aspiration, and their stature as lasting landmarks on neighborhood corners or country crossroads. These buildings tell stories; they are sites of community and congregational memories, rich with significant events in the lives of people who "belong" and others who have participated in one way or another.

   Too often, however, church buildings are viewed as an albatross and a liability. Many pastors see maintenance of church facilities as a huge time drain and beneath their higher calling to spread the faith. Many members exhibit an emotional attachment to their building that just frustrates pastors further. Some laity ally with pastors in arguing that spending money on buildings is sinful, diverting resources away from "mission," which usually seems to mean a ministry far away.

   But what if the building IS the mission? Not the mission itself, but the locus and enabler of effective mission. Isn't the mission of the church to serve the community, and by serving, to show others the visible reality of Christian faith? Constituents, pastors, district superintendents, and other denominational leaders need a conversion moment that will turn their pessimism about facilities into an asset-based outlook for seeing possibilities. But this change isn't going to happen unless (an interesting but effective segue to the next point):

2. People can shift from a ***private-property mentality*** to a ***public-facing asset perspective.*** Churches are as captive to the private-property mindset as any other part of American society.

Houses of worship are seen as extensions of the American dream: to own a house on a parcel of land for me, my family, and my possessions. Congregations become as protective as homeowners, anxious not to scratch the new flooring, fearful of strangers coming to the door, welcoming people but only friends and family.

Boards of trustees obtain insurance policies to cover losses usually based on replacement costs that can run into the millions. When the church loses its viability, the property is put on the market like any other house. But for houses of worship, the real estate listing can be a shock; their buildings are worth far less on the market than on an insurance policy. Meanwhile, the neighbors drive by, sadly shaking their heads to see another place of beauty and memory being sold.

The private-property mentality spins a web of assumptions around houses of worship just as tight as any other kind of building. It's hard to escape it. But what if congregations began to see the public-facing aspect of their buildings? Over the past several years, I have tracked the fate of the historic churches around Monument Square in the heart of a small New England city. I took a particular interest in First UMC, now with about thirty people in worship and rarely using their sanctuary that seated six hundred. Their building was insured for more than $2 million. When they decided to sell and merge with the local church in a nearby town, they were paid $125,000 for their gorgeous arts-and-crafts style building.

I don't live there and am not in a position to say what should have happened. What I observed was that the congregation was no longer connected to its community in any meaningful way. I was astounded to learn that the lay leader of the church had never met the mayor – in a town of thirteen-thousand people. Only one man in the congregation served on the board of any community organization. People at coffee hour were astonished when I told them that more than one stranger passing me on the sidewalk outside the church had noticed me looking at the building and commented how beautiful it was and how sad they were to see it getting a bit run-down. When the For Sale sign went up in the yard, many people in town were saddened and disappointed. But I wonder if anybody in the congregation even knew that.

When a congregation sees its building as private property and a maintenance burden they must bear alone, their perspective on the future just keeps shrinking. Once upon a time, they could take for granted their community connections because (so the myth goes) everybody went to church. They're simply not prepared to take initiative to build new community relationships. Many congregations, though, have the capacity to shift outlooks before resources run too low.

3. This shift in outlook requires a ***partnership paradigm.*** Congregations that see themselves as public-facing community assets are healthier and more likely to thrive – and most significant for this discussion, more able to maintain their facilities. They begin to see their buildings in a new light as the diverse and complex structures they are. Somewhat like public schools, churches have multiple spaces for a variety of functions: an auditorium, classrooms, a kitchen, dining area, sometimes a stage or performance space, or a gymnasium. Imagine these rooms without furnishings (with the exceptions of the kitchen and bathrooms). What possibilities are there with that kind of square footage and arrangement of rooms?

   An effective way to approach this is to set up a time for constituents of other community organizations to come see the building. A fresh set of eyes can help stir the congregation out of its taken-for-granted assumptions to see their rooms in a new way. Invite people from the business community – banks, chamber of commerce, civic clubs. Make sure constituents of nonprofit agencies are there – from the arts to education to social services of all kinds. Set up a process of continuing conversations about what the community needs, what could happen when groups partner together, how this space might be transformative for its neighborhood or town. Stifle all chatter about money; that's a topic that's only useful when there's a vision in place. Only when there's a compelling plan will there be any possibility of adequate funds falling into place.

This is only a sketch of what can happen when perspectives change. Annual conferences can advance by making resources available, through Partners for Sacred Places or other asset-based, community-development organizations. Instead of obsessing over numbers listed in district quarterly reports that go under the name "Vital Congregations," how about a set of questions that help congregations assess their buildings? What rooms does the building have? What is the square footage? How is each room being used? Are community groups welcome in your building? What partnerships do you have with other organizations in your community?

I chatted with a conference "congregational development" staff person recently, who understood the job to be all about starting new churches. Why is this? I suspect it's driven by a belief that only new churches will be effective in attracting new members. Meanwhile, the United Methodist Church has thousands of local churches needing fresh approaches to "development" that will connect them more effectively to their communities. Without this transformation, more and more historic houses of worship will have their only future in the real estate market. Every annual conference needs at least one staff member whose job description entails real estate. An additional staff member needs to be responsible for helping local churches get training in the wide opportunities available using an asset-based understanding of their properties and their potential.

In the last generation, the United Methodist Church as a denominational entity has been dragged down by fruitless membership campaigns and their companion piece of propping open local churches that lack a viable congregation at all. It's long past time to move on and face up to the denomination's real estate challenge.

Here is an excerpt of a 2009 real estate listing for the grand 1902 St. John's UMC in St. Louis:

BACK ON MARKET – PRICE REDUCED
Redevelopment opportunity – Unique Historic Structure – 41,018 square foot building on 1.55 acres of land.

Try your hand at writing a real estate listing for your church, describing it as thoroughly as you can. Now imagine: What can your local church, with the support and resources of your annual conference and district, do to convert this description with all its possibilities into new ministries and partnerships of church and community?

THOMAS EDWARD FRANK is University Professor Emeritus of Wake Forest University and author of *Historic Houses of Worship in Peril: Conserving Their Place in American Life* (Library Partners Press 2020).

Additional Resources

For more resources, see the Partners for Sacred Places website:

sacredplaces.org

Also, one of Partners for Sacred Places' emerging collaborations:

sacredplacescivicspaces.com

See also this enlightening interview with The Reverend Jacqueline Jones-Smith, pastor of the historic Christ Church UMC in downtown St. Petersburg, Florida, which adopted the asset-based approach:

churchleadership.com/leading-ideas/leveraging-your-churchs-assets

---

And don't miss these articles by Rick Reinhard, principal of Niagara Consulting Group. He led economic development organizations in five cities before shifting careers to work for the United Methodist Church in Washington DC and New Jersey:

On the UMC's real estate challenge and ways to approach it:

umnews.org/en/news/church-must-tackle-its-real-estate-crisis

On the rapidly growing number of vacant or underutilized houses of worship:

faithandleadership.com/
how-plan-the-post-pandemic-future-church-buildings

On new approaches and strategies for saving and redeveloping older houses of worship for community-serving ministries:

icma.org/articles/pm-magazine/redeveloping-houses-worship

CHAPTER FIFTEEN
From Heartbreak to Hollering for Change

Tori C. Butler

These are the words of Nehemiah, Hacaliah's son. In the month of Kislev, in the twentieth year while I was in the fortress city of Susa, ²Hanani, one of my brothers, came with some other men from Judah. I asked them about the Jews who had escaped and survived the captivity, and about Jerusalem.³ They told me, "Those in the province who survived the captivity are in great trouble and shame! The wall around Jerusalem is broken down, and its gates have been destroyed by fire!"⁴ When I heard this news, I sat down and wept. I mourned for days, fasting and praying before the God of heaven.

Nehemiah 1:1-4 CEB

This January, I started a sermon series at my church based on Dr. Joseph Daniels, Jr.'s book *Walking with Nehemiah: Your Community is Your Congregation*. He contends that for churches, communities, and individuals to find spiritual, physical, mental, financial, and relational wholeness in Jesus Christ, we must ask the question: "What or whom does our heart break for?"[1]

His question sparked an internal dialogue within me, and I have been ruminating on the following questions: What does my heart break for? Where did my heartbreak begin? Can anything be done about it?

To explore the question of what's next in the United Methodist Church, we must first name our heartbreak. Truthfully, depending on your social location and life experience, your heartbreak may be different than mine and mine different from yours. Yet, we know what it feels like to have our hearts broken, to have an experience that shakes our very foundation

---

1   Joseph Daniels, Jr., *Walking with Nehemiah: Your Community is Your Congregation*, Abingdon Press, 2014.

and brings us to our knees. We know what it feels like to have an experience that causes us to cry out to God from the depths of our beings.

We find Nehemiah, the cupbearer to the King of Babylon and the people of Judah, in the first chapter of the book of Nehemiah. The people of Judah know heartbreak. They have a history of being disconnected from their brothers and sisters because of internal strife and the worship of false idols. They have a history of being disconnected from God because of their idolatry and disobedience. Their disconnect with God ultimately led them into captivity, exiled in Babylon for seventy years.

During the time that the Judeans were captives in Babylon, Jerusalem was destroyed. Their temple, their place of worship, was no more. A quarter of the population now lived in occupied territory. Although displaced in Babylon, life was not too bad. Many lived as merchants and helped build the Babylonian economy. The exiled built their life in a foreign land. Yet, the memory of the death and destruction in Jerusalem never left them. Therefore, when the exile of the Jews was over, many returned home to Jerusalem to rebuild their lives. They restored their temple—the temple that Solomon built, the place where they believed the presence of God dwelled. They were trying to reclaim their identity. Part of the rebuilding process required people in both high and low places to get involved.

As the cupbearer to the king, Nehemiah held a trusted position. He was charged with watching the king's back and making sure no one poisoned him. He was essentially the king's butler. We can assume that Nehemiah's brother, Hanani, came with friends to visit him to tell Nehemiah about the destruction in Jerusalem and put pressure on him to do something about the circumstances. But before anyone could say anything, Nehemiah asked them what was going on. He wanted news about the Jews who escaped and survived the captivity.

What he found out devastated him. The scripture says, "Those in the province who survived the captivity are in great trouble and shame! The wall around Jerusalem is broken down, and its gates have been destroyed by fire!"[2] In other words, yes, the rebuilding process had started, but things were not going as planned. There was no protection for Jerusalem. There was no wall to fortify the city. Nothing was preventing the

---

[2] Nehemiah 1:3 (CEB).

tragedy of the exile from happening again. Nothing was stopping outside forces from destroying what they had rebuilt. The fact that pain and devastation were still going on in Jerusalem did something to Nehemiah. He sat down and wept. The scripture tells us he mourned for days. He fasted and prayed. Nehemiah, the one whose name means "The Lord Has Comforted,"[3] was in a place where he could not be consoled. He was made uncomfortable by the report he had received. God had broken his heart. Hearing the pain of his people did something to him.

Before the murder of George Floyd, there were two other incidents of racial injustice that broke my heart. The first was the death of Freddie Gray and the subsequent riots in Baltimore City. If you are unfamiliar with the story, Freddie was a 25-year-old Black man arrested for carrying a switchblade. He was placed inside a police transport van but never made it to his destination. Somehow his spinal cord was almost severed, and he was found unconscious. In essence, he died on the ride. His death in police custody caused an uproar in the community and led to protests and riots.

At the time, I was serving a church in East Texas and watching on TV as the city I was born and raised in was burning. I remember calling home and talking to my mother, who told me that the city was in lockdown and she was not allowed to leave her home. My heart did not just break for the loss of Freddie Gray that day, but it broke for my city. My heart broke for all those who, in the words of poet Dylan Thomas, were raging "… against the dying of the light."[4]

I believe the rioters and the protestors were raging not just because of the injustice of Freddie's death, but they were also raging because Freddie embodied their "somebodiness." Black theologian James Cone argues that "somebodiness" is this idea that Black folk can retain a sense of dignity even when they are treated as things. Therefore, if Freddie's body and Freddie's life did not matter because he was just another young Black man in Baltimore, then what does that say about all the other young Black bodies and their personhood. Let's just say my heart still breaks about this.

---

[3] Daniels, 4.

[4] Dylan Thomas, "Do Not Go Gentle into that Good Night," *The Poems of Dylan Thomas,* New Directions, 2003.

The second incident of racial injustice that still angers and frustrates me was the death of Philando Castille. (Yes, I know it is dangerous to admit that I feel anger as a Black woman, but it is the emotion I feel every time I think of what happened.) Philando was pulled over in a suburb of Minneapolis-St. Paul, Minnesota. Some reports say it was for a broken taillight and others say because he supposedly resembled a suspect in a robbery. Nevertheless, he was pulled over with his girlfriend and a toddler in the car. He alerted the police that he did have a weapon in the car. The police officer shot at Philando seven times, hitting him five times. He died in the car with his girlfriend and toddler present.

My heartbreak starts with the fact that in the video his girlfriend posted on social media, you can hear the toddler trying to comfort her mother and de-escalate the situation. In what world should a four-year-old have to try to make sense of the insensible? My heart broke because Philando alerted the police of the possible danger to him, the officer. Philando does everything to make sure those around him are safe, but the police do not do the same. The officer shot in a car with a toddler inside. It was broadcasted for the world to see, for the church to see. In that moment, we were invited into the pain and cries of a young mother and a toddler. We were invited into a moment of lament.

Lament is crying out to God and expecting God to respond. It is a moment of giving voice to pain with the expectation that something can be done about it. But this was more than just lament; it is what scholar A. Elaine Brown Crawford would call "The Holler." "The holler is the primal cry of pain, abuse, violence, separation... [and] the renunciation of racialized and genderized violence."[5] As United Methodists, we are charged to lament and holler. When we are baptized, this question is posed: "Do you accept the freedom and power God gives you to resist evil, injustice, and oppression in whatever forms they present themselves?"[6] Sometimes the larger church misses out on the fact that we profess that we will call out and cry out against injustice and oppression, and that means we are charged to cry out against the injustice perpetrated against black, brown, and native bodies. We cannot be silent. We cannot falter in hollering for change in this aspect of our society. It is who we say we are.

---

[5] A. Elaine Brown Crawford, *Hope in the Holler: A Womanist Theology,* Westminster John Knox Press, 2002.

[6] "Baptismal Covenant I," Discipleship Ministries, accessed February 5, 2022, https://www.umcdiscipleship. org/book-of-worship/the-baptismal-covenant-i.

I truly believe that we cannot holler for systemic change in the United Methodist Church regarding human sexuality if we are not willing to holler for change in how black, brown, and native bodies are being unfairly treated. Being the church requires us to acknowledge that hearts are not just broken over the issue of human sexuality, but hearts are broken by the fact that we are not living into who we say we are. Hearts are broken by the fact that the church is not fully addressing its complicity in perpetuating racial violence. Hearts are broken by the fact that we are not using this moment in history to rewrite our narrative as a church. In other words, what's next can be a season where we are not just hollering for change in the issue of human sexuality, but we are also intentionally hollering for change in the treatment of black, brown, and native bodies in the pulpit, pew, and public square.

The Northeastern Jurisdiction "Call to Action on Racial Justice" on the Baltimore-Washington Conference's website offers some practical ways to live into the change. There you will find tremendous resources in how to engage in anti-racism work and read about Rev. Brian Tillman's work on racial reconciliation. There is so much information out there on how to engage in racial justice work.

Yet, everything starts with heartbreak. What I love about lament is that it is individual and communal. That means we are called to enter each other's pain. We are called to cry out to God together. I pray that as you read my words and feel my pain, you will be led to lament, to holler for change in the issue of racial justice, too!

Rev. Dr. Tori Butler is senior pastor of Asbury Town Neck United Methodist Church in Severna Park, Maryland. Before moving to Maryland, she served three cross-cultural appointments in the Texas Annual Conference of The United Methodist Church.

In 2020, she was invited to speak at the 57th Anniversary of the March on Washington. Dr. Butler is a contributor to *Do Not Be Afraid: Bishops & Young Clergy Share Signs of Resurrection & Words of Hope* and *I'm Black. I'm Christian. I'm Methodist.*

CHAPTER SIXTEEN
You Can't Ruin the Church

Ryan G. Spurrier

"Don't worry. You can't ruin the church. Christ will preserve the church. You can't ruin it." Bishop Ken Carder kindly spoke these words to our class after watching the reactions of third-year divinity students as a guest lecturer shared how hard it can be to mobilize a local congregation for mission. These students were acutely aware that they would be responsible for leading a church in just a matter of months. So, each time the lecturer shared another difficulty, they sank a little lower and a little lower in their desks, their faces becoming a little longer and a little longer.

Bishop Carder, the consummate pastor who would always stop class to offer wisdom and care, took note. When the guest left the room, he reassured us, "You can't ruin the church. Christ will preserve the church." But then, with a playful grin, he continued, "You might ruin a few local congregations. But, not the church."

I have recalled this scene from class many times during the three years since the 2019 General Conference. Previously, I had always taken it as a lesson about my individual location of ministry, but now it rings true for the denomination. Christ is much more concerned with preserving the church than any particular expression of it. As Jeremiah proclaimed of old, whether we are preserved has little to do with what logo we hang on our door and everything to do with whether we are being faithful (Cf. Jeremiah 7:1-15). Christ will preserve faithfulness. The question is simply whether that will include us.

To be completely honest with you, I do not know what the future of the United Methodist Church will be or should be. I am not someone who is often invited into, nor do I seek out, high-level conversations or negotiations. I find that being a campus minister itself demands more time than I can offer.

But, I do know my students – my particular students had not asked about General Conference at all in the months leading up to it. It was not on their radars, but after it began, they got sucked in by its drama and were deeply hurt and disillusioned equally by its process and final votes. Watching the debates and votes, they sat with blank eyes. Not moving. Not speaking.

I was disillusioned, too. Although disheartened is a more accurate word because I knew that what was playing out in St. Louis was just another example of how we have been treating each other in the United Methodist Church for a while.

Everything in my spiritual formation and theological training screams that we are going about this all wrong. We seem content with the false peace of convincing ourselves that 51% voting for our side is faithfulness and something to be proud of. We seem to have forgotten how to listen to, love, and live with people we do not agree with. Growing up, I was taught that these were hallmarks of the United Methodist Church. Others would look at our Sunday school classes and wonder how people from such different world views could live together week after week. And yet, we used to know how.

We seem to have forgotten that Jesus said that how we treat our enemies and the people we do not agree with says more about our faith than how we treat the people we like (Cf. Luke 6:32-36). We rationalize that we have, indeed, cared for the least of these if we help the "poor" – however we define that term to include the people we are comfortable enough helping – without ever questioning how we treat the people we think the least of. Yet, Jesus left us no loopholes to treat people poorly just because we do not share their beliefs, even if we find those beliefs repulsive.[1] Even the person dismissed from the church in Mathew 18 is to be treated as a Gentile and a tax collector, the very people Jesus lovingly seeks out.[2]

---

[1] This paragraph is indebted to Will D. Campbell, "Speech to the Southern Baptist Theological Seminary," *Writings on Reconciliation and Resistance*, Richard C. Goode, ed., Cascade Books, 2010.

[2] This idea is indebted to chapter titled, "The Saints," Dietrich Bonhoeffer, *Discipleship, Dietrich Bonhoeffer Works, vol. 4*, Fortress Press, 2001.

We seem to have forgotten that original sin is a misplaced desire to definitively know what is good and what is evil so that we can then arbitrate who is good and who is evil, almost always excusing ourselves to point fingers at others.[3] Did anyone else notice the apple sitting on the podium beside Bishop Harvey as the final votes were tallied at General Conference? It broke my heart.

It broke my heart because my faith came of age in a dorm room at Clemson University, in the northwest corner of South Carolina. I, a white man, shared this same room with the same roommate, an African American man, for four years. Our window looked out on an old plantation house as we learned, through our relationship, that there is still so much in our society that would keep us apart. There was so much we had to unlearn about the way society had taught us to interact with each other in order for us to learn how to love each other. In that process, our common ground was our Christian faith.

Our relationship was not very common on our campus in the mid-2000s. Looking back, I realize that the most profound lesson I learned while living with my roommate was that if our shared faith had nothing to say in the face of all the social forces that would keep us apart, it meant nothing. But, if it did have something to say, then it meant everything.

As we began to live out the truth that, in Christ Jesus, society's dividing walls are already torn down, our faith came alive in ways we could never have imagined (Cf. Ephesians 2:14-18). As we began to invite our friends to join us, we all began to experience the Holy Spirit's presence in increasingly powerful ways. In short, we found salvation.

These experiences compelled me into ministry, but they also demanded a new theological footing to guard against self-righteous pride. How would we guard ourselves against demonizing those who also called themselves Christian but either did not see – or saw no problem with – white supremacy? My campus minister introduced us to the sixth chapter of Ephesians: "For our struggle is not against enemies of blood and flesh, but against the rulers, against the authorities, against the cosmic powers of this present darkness, against the spiritual forces

---

[3] This idea is indebted to "Matthew 7: The Community of Disciples Is Set Apart (The Disciple and the Unbelievers)," Dietrich Bonhoeffer, *Discipleship, Dietrich Bonhoeffer Works, vol. 4*, Fortress Press, 2001.

of evil in the heavenly places" (Eph. 6:12, NRSV). He introduced us to Ubuntu theology, teaching us that our humanity is inextricably bound to everyone else's humanity, for we can only be human together.

If we ever got this wrong, if we ever forgot and instead took the seemingly easier path of thinking that other people are our enemies instead of staying focused on deeper, spiritual systems of oppression, it would harm our own souls. If we gave in to the temptation to dehumanize those persons who would try to dehumanize us, we would, in fact, dehumanize ourselves, for our own humanity depends on nothing short of demanding the full humanity of every other person.

Believing that the heart of Jesus' Gospel is more concerned with how we treat those we think the least of instead of how we treat those we like, I was disheartened by the 2019 General Conference. Again, I was not disillusioned because we have not been treating each other well for a while now.

But, my students were disillusioned. The process was all new to them, at least when it came to their church. Several years ago, while watching my students attempt to make sense of the political realities in which they are coming of age, I realized that every political memory they have comes after the previously inconceivable act of a member of the US House of Representatives calling the President a liar during the State of the Union Address. They have seen nothing other than entrenched partisanship with ever-decreasing levels of decorum and civility. They expected their church to do better, but as is too often the case, their church reflected the wider culture instead of modeling a more excellent way.

And so, they were disillusioned – but only for a few days until their resolve was settled and consistent: "General Conference was wrong, but I know that it does not represent my community at UNC Wesley." Some even began a semantic protest of their own, referring to themselves as Method-ish. They were not going to leave their Methodist campus ministry or their Wesleyan roots, but they were not sure they wanted to commit to all that goes with United Methodism these days. For some, the "-ish" gave them enough of a loophole.

Of course, we have plenty of logs in our own eyes at UNC Wesley. Our average student would consider themselves progressive on every issue you can imagine, but our community does not yet embody Christ's hospitality: Our racial diversity is nowhere near the demographics of our university, LGBTQ+ students are not as open about their sexuality within Wesley as in other communities on campus, and we still fall to the temptation of wanting to be right more than we care about those we believe to be wrong. But, we are learning to see these logs and are desiring to be better.

To be frank, few of my students are invested in whether the United Methodist Church remains intact or even if it remains a denomination. But, they are deeply invested in how our community can more fully reflect and usher in the Kingdom of God on our campus.

Will the United Methodist Church still be here in five years or fifty? I do not know. Will UNC Wesley Campus Ministry still be here in five years or fifty? I do not know that either, but I do know that Christ will sustain the places where faithfulness flourishes.

I do believe that if we can get out of our own way and let the Holy Spirit teach us again how to resist that original temptation of being overly fascinated with arbitrating what is good and what is evil and if we can let the Spirit teach us to care more about loving those we disagree with than getting 51% of the vote, then Christ will sustain us. As a bonus, we will almost certainly discover a deeper understanding of faithfulness that will surprise all of us in ways we do not expect.

But, if we cannot reclaim Christian character amid our disagreements, then perhaps we are already the grain of wheat that must fall into the earth so that God can build something new (Cf. John 12:24).

Rev. Ryan G. Spurrier is campus minister and executive director of Wesley Campus Ministry at the University of North Carolina at Chapel Hill. A product of campus ministry himself, Ryan loves forming and shaping young adults for Christian leadership, both as clergy and laity. He believes that life becomes abundant when our lives are aligned with God's desire that all creation flourishes.

CHAPTER SEVENTEEN
What's Next in United Methodist Education

Christopher Donald

When I was just a child, nearly forty years ago, I remember a special Sunday at my home church in western Virginia. In my memory, Bishop Stockton was visiting and preaching that day, but we had another visitor as well, a representative from Randolph-Macon College. At the offering, the RMC rep stood up and described the work of the college, concluding with the declaration, "Randolph-Macon is YOUR college!" And then we passed the offering plate twice: once, as usual, for our congregation, and once for OUR college, Randolph-Macon. And people gave generously. And that wasn't all. Several of my friends from church attended Randolph-Macon. After all, we were United Methodists, and Randolph-Macon was OUR college in Virginia.

Decades later, as the chaplain at Millsaps College, I traveled around Mississippi for a different reason. The college had developed a reputation as a place that challenged the religious and political values of United Methodist young adults. I was assuring skeptical congregations that we would be good stewards of their apportionment dollars and that we would nurture and care for their young people. I talked about stories of freedom in the Bible and how Millsaps was an institution committed to freedom. My framing of the college's mission in terms of our Christian faith sometimes won over doubtful congregants and reluctant applicants.

My experiences, some thirty-five years apart, demonstrate significant changes in the higher education institutions of the United Methodist Church in the United States, in higher education in the United States more generally, and in the United Methodist denomination. The United

Methodist Church is confronting its most serious challenge in decades: the conflict over whether full inclusion of members and leaders who identify with LGBTQI+ communities will divide the church. At the same time, United Methodist institutions of higher education are at a critical juncture. When compared with other colleges and universities, the United Methodist institutions are confronting existential challenges, including rising costs, declining enrollment, declining enrollment of diverse students, and falling completions, especially for diverse students.

In this chapter, we will review the history and purpose of higher education in the Methodist movement; take a snapshot of our United Methodist institutions and context of higher education in the United States; then consider the possible futures of United Methodist colleges and universities.

Purposes of United Methodist Education

The founding legend of the Methodist movement takes place on a university campus: young men at Oxford University gathered in a "Holy Club" with a systematic way of embodying faith in practices of devotion, prayer, service, and accountability. So it makes sense that, as the Methodist movement grew, our people established institutions of higher education. These institutions offered a unique Wesleyan worldview, manifesting the importance of both reason and faith for effective service to the church and the world. Today, United Methodist institutions also explicitly support diverse student bodies and the inclusion of all students in campus communities. Those foundational principles continue to influence the nature of United Methodist higher education today.

Knowledge and Faith

One reason Methodists formed colleges was to instruct young people in shared Wesleyan values and worldview. At the founding of the first Methodist school in 1748, Charles Wesley penned a hymn that stated the mission to "Unite the pair so long disjoined, Knowledge and vital piety; Learning and holiness combined." This dual commitment remains at the heart of United Methodist higher education. As West Virginia Wesleyan College confirms in their mission statement, "The College is a community of learning based on fundamental principles formed at the intersection of Christian faith and liberal education." At its best, this Wesleyan worldview meant a commitment to a generous and loving Christian life, engaged with the world, and in service to others.

The pursuit of knowledge requires academic freedom – the freedom to question, explore, and discover – for faculty and students. In the United Methodist Social Principles, the General Conference affirms that United Methodist institutions "... ensure that academic freedom is protected for all members of the academic community and a learning environment is fostered that allows for a free exchange of ideas." This means education at a United Methodist institution is also nonsectarian, unhindered by any religious requirements to join the community of scholars or dogmatic limitations on academic inquiry.

But what sets United Methodist institutions apart – and the gift we offer in the broader system of American higher education – is the parallel and equally important concern with the spiritual development of students. In the 19th century, this meant making students into good Wesleyans; by the mid-20th century, into good Protestant Christians. It is impossible to assume any religious identity for students today. Yet, United Methodist institutions are dedicated to the idea that humans are inherently spiritual beings. That is to say, people are created to reflect on who they are (identity), what they believe (faith), their place in the world (relationships and community), and how to make choices about their lives because of their beliefs (morals and ethics).

Ohio Northern University shows this commitment to nonsectarian spiritual development by affirming that they "welcome persons of all faiths by providing a supportive environment for their moral and spiritual growth." While broader conceptions of academic freedom and spiritual development are the norm today, United Methodist colleges and universities continue to offer students – as the Wesleys did at the very first Methodist school – the joining of academic inquiry that is rigorous and free with spiritual growth as reflective, engaged, and generous people.

Service in the World

Perhaps the most significant reason Methodists established schools and colleges was that communities and the church needed educated leaders. In the early 19th century, the Methodist Episcopal Church was expanding rapidly. Clergy and laity had to be educated to practice personal piety and to lead growing congregations, conferences, and mission organizations. But Methodist-educated laity also became community leaders. Emory & Henry College, named for a church leader, Bishop John Emory, and a civil leader, Patrick Henry, was founded "upon the principles of vital faith and civic engagement." At the same time, Methodist laity and clergy often lived in places beyond the reach of governmental authority or under a government uninterested in education. In these cases, Methodists established schools and colleges to educate their children and young adults. Willamette University, the oldest institution of higher education in the western United States, was founded in 1842 as a pre-collegiate school serving the children of missionaries and settlers. The need for education of children and young adults who could serve their communities and the church was another reason Methodists established schools and colleges.

Nineteenth-century Methodist institutions were dedicated to preparing students for service in the Methodist denominations or particular geographic regions. Today, United Methodist colleges and universities prepare students to serve as leaders in their communities, as good citizens in our democratic polity, and as active participants in a global society. Iowa Wesleyan College pledges that its commitment to spiritual values and community leads to "... civic engagement and service to one another." Centenary University acknowledges its role in preparing students for leadership in the regional and global context.

Some institutions also use language that reflects current social concerns to describe the scope and impact of the service they encourage. For instance, in its mission statement, Illinois Wesleyan College declares its commitment to "... diversity, social justice, and environmental sustainability." Service to others, reimagined for a democratic society, global context, and addressing current social challenges, continues to be a central element of United Methodist higher education.

Commitments to Diversity and Inclusion

At the same time, Methodists founded institutions that reflected worldly values. Separation based on race or gender was the norm in

American society in the 19th and most of the 20th century, and Methodists, for the most part, did not challenge it. For example, Willamette University, mentioned above, was founded to serve white children; another school was established for Native American children by the same Methodist missionaries. Colleges were also established for Black or African American students and for women, though often without the material support, academic rigor, or prestige of the colleges for white men. Building colleges for these excluded constituencies was likely viewed as progressive at the time, even though we now understand that this "separate and unequal" was contrary to both Christian and Wesleyan values.

United Methodist colleges and universities no longer enforce such social divisions, and many are confronting their prejudiced pasts while embracing the diversity and inclusion necessary to manifest true Christian community and provide an outstanding educational experience. Willamette is now an institution with deep commitment to diversity and inclusion and embraces and celebrates all identities, including the celebration of the Native American culture indigenous to the region.

Dillard University, a historically Black university, was founded in 1930 from merging predecessor institutions established by white missionaries to serve formerly enslaved people. Dillard, the vision of Black leaders in New Orleans, was reestablished on a commitment to educate Black and African American students through a liberal arts curriculum (an explicit rejection of the vocational education that was often typical for Black students at the time) and to engage with the Black community beyond campus through extension programs and clubs. Even institutions founded upon prejudiced assumptions have left behind those intentions and embraced the importance of diversity and inclusion as an indispensable part of their higher education mission.

The work of reflection on past actions and prejudiced intentions continues. Many United Methodist colleges and universities are still examining their history to understand how their actions were guided, not by the Christian virtue of love but by unjust, worldly values. One relevant aspect of this work is the inclusion of individuals who identify with LGBTQI+ communities. United Methodist colleges and universities include explicit statements of full acceptance and inclusion of LGBTQI+ identifying individuals, among other diverse identities. For most institutional leaders, this is merely an extension of their schools' mission to allow freedom of thought and nonsectarian spiritual development.

For some, full inclusion of members of LGBTQI+ communities and other diverse identities is a manifestation of the final, fully reconciled vision God holds for humanity. But that stance has placed many United Methodist institutions at odds with the church, conferences, congregations, and individual members. As my experience with Millsaps College demonstrates, this friction reinforces the sense that colleges and the church are working towards different objectives. Truth-telling about our institutions' histories and current struggles with diversity and inclusion is necessary to begin a process of reconciliation and realignment with the Wesleyan commitment to join "knowledge and vital piety" for loving service to others.

The work of education began in the Methodist movement to "unite the pair so long disjoined, knowledge and vital piety," to the end that good works could be done in the world by serving others. That vision continues in United Methodist higher education today, with affirmations of academic freedom in the pursuit of knowledge by faculty and students, emphasizing spiritual development and growth, and service in terms of citizenship and participation in global society. While Methodist higher education sometimes reflected the unjust and oppressive values of the world, today's explicit commitments to campus diversity, inclusion, and celebration of all identities are typical.

Context and Snapshot

Higher education in the United States is incredibly diverse, perhaps more so than in other countries. The triple purpose of higher education – research, teaching, and service – is embodied differently in every institution. This incredibly complex system is the context in which United Methodist higher education institutions operate.

For this chapter, I employ data from the National Center for Education Statistics (NECS) based on institutional reporting in the Integrated Postsecondary Education Data System (IPEDS) and the framework established in the Carnegie Classification of Institutions of Higher Education. Using these tools, I limit the types of United Methodist and other institutions in this analysis. The 109 United Methodist institutions under the supervision of the General Board of Higher Education and Ministry include secondary schools, colleges educating undergraduates with liberal arts and professional curricula, major research universities, and specialized professional schools. However, most United Methodist colleges and universities serve undergraduates primarily, providing education in the liberal arts or professions.

Universities classified as "Doctoral Universities—Very High Research Activity" (R1) and "Doctoral Universities—High Research Activity" (R2) are eliminated from the analysis, as are the theological and medical schools – so-called "Special Focus Four-Year" schools – and the handful of "Associate's Colleges." There are no United Methodist "Special Focus Two-Year" schools or private, for-profit institutions. Institutions classified as "Doctoral/Professional Universities" (D/PU) are retained, as are "Master's Colleges and Universities" (M1, M2, and M3), so long as the enrollment profile is "majority undergraduate," "high undergraduate," "very high undergraduate," or "exclusively undergraduate." A list of 75 United Methodist institutions from across the United States, serving primarily undergraduates, remains.

I also created a cohort of "peer" institutions for comparison to include private, not-for-profit, four-year institutions classified as Baccalaureate Colleges, M1, M2, M3, or D/PU with an enrollment profile of "majority undergraduate," "high undergraduate," "very high undergraduate," or "exclusively undergraduate." The peer cohort also excludes Associate's Colleges, R1/2 institutions, Special Focus Two- and Four-Year schools, and private, for-profit institutions. This results in a cohort of 776 institutions which are compared to the similarly-situated United Methodist cohort.

I also developed a "sector" cohort intended to capture more broadly trends in American higher education. The sector cohort includes public and private, not-for-profit institutions. It also includes Baccalaureate Colleges, M1, M2, M3, D/PU, and R1/2 institutions, while eliminating private, for-profit schools, Associate's Colleges, and Special Focus Two- and Four-Year schools. There is no restriction on the enrollment profile for the sector cohort, resulting in a sector cohort of 1,542 colleges and universities.

The issues that American higher education is confronting are varied, but several stand out as especially significant. Most recently, the COVID-19 pandemic has accelerated the expected and emerging trend of declining total enrollment. Almost any article or book on American higher education recognizes several additional challenges: rising costs and affordability, failure to enroll diverse students, low completion rates, and even lower completion rates for diverse students. This is the context in which United Methodist higher education institutions operate and the set of challenges that they face as well.

Pricing, Cost of Attendance, and Affordability

The rising cost of attendance concerns both students and higher education leaders. The National Center for Education Statistics (NCES) reported that in the 2018-19 academic year, undergraduate tuition, fees, room, and board were estimated to be $18,383 at public institutions and $47,419 at private, non-profit institutions. In the decade from 2008-09 to 2018-19, the cost of attendance increased 28% at public institutions and by 19% at private, not-for-profit institutions when adjusted for inflation.

In 2010 the average total cost to attend a United Methodist institution was $35,887, and in 2020 that average total cost was $48,888, an increase of 36%; but this increase is only 12.5% when calculated in 2020 dollars. In this case, the increases in cost seem moderate from a student perspective (though still far outstripping inflation for other services). However, issues of cost from an institutional perspective are still problematic when it comes to enrolling students and covering operational costs.

Though tuition increases are less when controlled for inflation, United Methodist institutions confront the same challenges as other schools regarding cost. The quality or added value of a college degree is difficult for students and their families to assess, particularly because the added value of a college degree is spread throughout a student's lifetime of earning and other intangible outcomes (college graduates are healthier, live longer, have better relationships, etc.).

The only real metric students and families possess to measure the quality and value of their education is the price that other students and families are willing to pay. This incentivizes institutions to price their tuition and other expenses as high as possible since higher tuition presumably indicates the quality of the education offered by an institution. Unfortunately, studies show that a high cost of attendance ("sticker price") deters students from applying to a college, especially students from lower socioeconomic backgrounds or racial or ethnic minorities. Institutions attempt to counterbalance this by offering institutional aid to offset cost, but many diverse students, seeing the initial "sticker price," choose not to pursue enrollment.

This employment of institutional aid to induce enrollment also complicates the work of institutional leaders because those students who do accept institutional aid and enroll are not receiving a funded award (that is to say, one in which an endowment or third party is actually paying tuition to the institution) but a discount (a reduction in price in which the institution assumes the loss). In 2020, 95.5% of students enrolled at a United Methodist institution received an institutional grant with an average award of $21,296, often an unfunded award. For example, an institution with a sticker price of $45,000 may discount tuition $20,000 to entice a student to enroll. So the institution ends up receiving only $25,000 in tuition from that student (probably from the federal government in the form of grants and loans), which may barely cover the actual cost to the institution of that student's education. Multiply this across four classes of undergraduate students, and an institution could be in a precarious financial position, dependent on securing every possible dollar from tuition and fees.

In summary, rising costs of attendance create a challenge for students, and they may never pursue applying or enrolling. At the same time, higher education leaders must discount tuitions through unfunded grants undercutting institutional financial well-being.

While not directly connected to the cost of attendance, declining support by annual and jurisdictional conferences and the General Conference also influence the financial well-being of United Methodist institutions. Data on these actual dollar amounts provided to United Methodist institutions are reported in individual conference journals. Establishing trend data would mean reviewing several years of journals for dozens of conferences. Suffice it to say that the tens of thousands or even hundreds of thousands of dollars in grants from conferences are a small fraction of what United Methodist institutions take in from tuition and fees or annual charitable contributions.

The reasons for the declining monetary support to United Methodist institutions are difficult to define with data. Anecdotal evidence would suggest that congregations and conferences, faced with declining and aging memberships and obligated to the costs associated with aging buildings and healthcare and retirement liabilities, have chosen to reduce support for higher education. The decline in United Methodist support for our institutions is unfortunate, but the reality is that United Methodist colleges are tuition-driven institutions. The tension between sticker price and actual cost and the effect pricing has on student decisions, particularly diverse students, to apply or enroll are what concern institutional leaders and should concern church leaders as well.

Enrollment and Diversity

Enrollment data show that more students and more diverse students than ever before are enrolling in American colleges and universities. The peer cohort saw enrollment from 2010 to 2020 increase by 14%, while the sector cohort enrollment grew by 9% in the same period. These students are also more diverse. The peer cohort enrolled nearly twice as many students identifying as two or more races and more than doubled the number of students identifying as Hispanic or Latino. Peer institutions also enrolled 41% more students identifying as Asian and 13% more students identifying as Black or African American. The Pell Grant, offered by the federal government to low-income students, serves as a reasonable proxy for socioeconomic diversity. In the peer cohort, about 34% of students received a Pell Grant, a number that has remained fairly steady since 2010. The sector cohort shows similar trends in the diverse identities of students enrolling, both in race/ethnicity and socioeconomic status.

The data on enrollment and diversity in United Methodist institutions is more complicated. Total enrollment in United Methodist institutions declined by 13% between 2010 and 2020, with the steepest declines in 2019 (3%) and 2020 (4%). The enrollment of students identifying with diverse communities has declined for some groups and increased for others. From 2010 to 2020, the number of students identifying as two or more races increased 131%, students identifying as Hispanic or Latino increased 81%, and students identifying as Asian increased 9%.

At the same time, the number of students identifying as Black or African American decreased by 12%, and students identifying as

American Indian or Alaska Native and Native Hawaiian or Other Pacific Islander decreased by 25% and 29%, respectively. In 2020, 38.7% of students enrolled at United Methodist institutions received a Pell Grant. This number is slightly down from 2010, when 40.2% of students received a Pell Grant.

Though the composition of diverse populations has changed, the proportion of diverse students to overall enrollment has remained relatively flat and even increased. However, the absolute decline in the enrollment of racially, ethnically, and socioeconomically diverse students means the campuses of United Methodist institutions are also less diverse.

(I also examined trends in gender of enrolled students over the 2010 to 2020 period for United Methodist, peer, and sector institutions. The gender proportion remained stable over that time in all three cohorts. Another important note is that NECS and almost all institutions collect data only on traditional, binary gender identities.)

It is difficult to say for sure, without more sophisticated statistical analysis than this, why these trends are the way they are. Certainly, the COVID-19 pandemic has something to do with recent fluctuations. Changes in federal financial aid policies across presidential administrations have also influenced students' decisions about higher education. Some changes to the enrollment of diverse students, particularly students identifying as Hispanic or two or more races, reflect changes in demographic and social perspectives. But the steady declines, and then the more rapid recent declines, in total enrollment and in certain diverse constituencies also coincide with the controversies in the United Methodist Church over the place and role of church members and leaders who identify with LGBTQI+ communities.

Signals of exclusion of some diverse groups (LGBTQI+ communities) by the United Methodist Church may have had a dilatory effect on whether members of other diverse groups (racial, ethnic, socioeconomic, etc.) are willing to apply to and enroll in United Methodist-affiliated institutions. The National Center for Education Statistics and most institutions do not collect information on LGBTQI+ identities, so it is difficult to say how the conflict in the church has affected whether or not students identifying with those communities enrolled at United Methodist institutions.

One final consideration affecting enrollment is the "church-to-college" pipeline. A once-steady flow of students from United Methodist congregations, youth groups, and camps to United Methodist colleges and universities and campus ministries has ended. I found statistics on youth church members reported in the voluminous statistical tables of the journals of my annual conference—reported by congregation but not in aggregate. And, if my brief survey of data in the most recent journal from my home conference, district, and congregation is any indication, most of those data are incorrect.

At the same time, I could not find a United Methodist institution that published how many enrolled students identify as United Methodist, if that data is collected at all. Given broader trends in mainline denominations and denominational colleges, I suspect that the United Methodist Church has fewer youth to send to United Methodist institutions of higher education, and United Methodist institutions are enrolling few United Methodist students. In any case, even as enrollment and diverse enrollment at peer and sector institutions increases, enrollment at United Methodist institutions is declining, as is the number of diverse students on campus.

Completion Rates

One measure of whether institutions are achieving their objective of educating and graduating students is student completions. Student completion is assessed by the number of students finishing a degree within 150% of the time to degree (for a bachelor's degree, six years), known as a six-year graduation rate. For United Methodist institutions, the six-year graduation rate for the cohort that enrolled in fall 2010 was 56.8%, and for the cohort that enrolled in fall 2014, it was 57.9%, a very small change over time. At the same time, the six-year graduation rate for peer institutions rose slightly from 60.9% for the fall 2010 cohort to 62.9% for the fall 2014 cohort. The sector cohort fared slightly better still, with the fall 2010 cohort completing at a rate of 61.4% and the fall 2014 cohort completing at 64.9%.

One particularly concerning data point is the completion rate of Black or African American students, particularly Black men. In the sector cohort, Black students graduate within six years about 40% of the time.

In the peer cohort, Black students in the fall 2010 cohort graduated at a rate of 37.9%; that rose significantly to 44.2% in the fall 2014 cohort. However, at United Methodist institutions, Black or African American students completed a bachelor's degree in six years at rates of 35.9% (fall 2010 cohort) and 36.6% (fall 2014 cohort). And if Black men are the emphasis, the rates are more discouraging: less than one in three Black men enrolled in the fall 2010 and fall 2014 cohorts graduated from a United Methodist institution with a bachelor's degree. The reasons a student does not persist to completion varies by individual, but research suggests major obstacles have to do with lack of a sense of belonging or community on campus, financial limitations, outside or family obligations, and academic challenges.

It may be that the conflict in the church over full inclusion of members and leaders identifying with LGBTQI+ communities also communicates to members of other minority or marginalized communities that they might not be welcomed at United Methodist institutions either. At the very least, this data on completions suggests that United Methodist institutions, working with reduced resources, may not meet the needs of their students, particularly minority students, when it comes to making the campus a welcoming and inclusive community and making higher education an achievable reality for all students.

Possible Futures

The review of the purposes and statistics on United Methodist institutions of higher education is intended to express one point: our colleges and universities were facing existential challenges even before disagreement over the place and role of LGBTQI+-community members in the United Methodist Church spilled out into open conflict and inevitable schism. It is difficult to project the possible future of individual institutions because so much is dependent on factors distinct to each institution. It does seem undeniable that the United Methodist Church's likely division is not helping our institutions. However, there are several possibilities for the future of Methodist institutions, including broadening the base of support, selling to or merging with another institution, and leaving church affiliate status.

Broadening the Base

The institutions considered in this chapter almost exclusively serve undergraduates on residential campuses, an expensive, resource-intense education. It requires the construction and maintenance of classroom and laboratory buildings for various disciplines, libraries, technology infrastructure, residence halls, dining facilities, and other student-serving facilities like health clinics and athletics facilities. It requires money to staff, run, and service these facilities. Institutions that can find a way to spread the cost across more students, especially students who do not use campus facilities every day, can control costs more effectively.

One institution that has redistributed cost well is High Point University in High Point, North Carolina. Thirty years ago, High Point was an institution like many other United Methodist schools – a small, residential, undergraduate-focused, liberal arts college struggling to attract students, maintain aging facilities, and pay the bills. Since the early 2000s, High Point has transformed into an institution offering various practical, professional programs to undergraduate and graduates with the liberal arts at its core. Most importantly, this expansion of graduate programs has enabled High Point to spread the cost of education across students.

Evening and online programs in professional fields are less expensive to provide than traditional undergraduate education, yet those evening and online programs charge full tuition with very little unfunded discounting. At the same time, the expansion of graduate, professional programs enhances offerings for undergraduates. Undergraduate majors in business, engineering, education, and communications are available alongside traditional liberal arts majors in sciences, arts, humanities, and social sciences that have been made career-oriented through real-world experiences like service learning, internships, and study abroad. These additional offerings are attractive to students who will spend tens of thousands of dollars for their education, including taking on debt through student loans. Since High Point began this aggressive expansion of graduate offerings and undergraduate career-oriented education in 2005, traditional undergraduate enrollment has increased from 2,500 to 5,600.

Of course, this model of transformation is not without risk. High Point invested deeply in physical facilities and in luring the best talent to begin

166

these schools and programs, sometimes through gifts and sometimes through debt instruments. In addition, High Point's United Methodist identity is not immediately evident in publications, and it is unclear from strategic and other documents whether spiritual development remains an institutional priority. Still, this broadening of the base has made it possible for High Point to continue fulfilling its mission to educate and serve. High Point now enrolls more and more diverse students, and it also functions as an economic engine for a region that has been devastated by the loss of manufacturing industries over the last three decades.

Sale or Merger

In the last decade, two United Methodist institutions in Tennessee have opted to sell themselves to state institutions. After struggling with financial and accreditation problems, Lambuth University in Jackson, Tennessee, opted to close in 2011. After operations concluded, the campus was sold to the University of Memphis, the primary state university in western Tennessee, which now operates the Jackson campus as the University of Memphis—Lambuth. Rather than closing and simply selling the physical plant, Martin Methodist College, located in Pulaski, Tennessee, recently merged into the University of Tennessee system, becoming the University of Tennessee Southern. This merger ensured that faculty, students, and staff could remain as a community on the Pulaski campus. In fact, tuition for students is expected to decrease by nearly 60%.

There are advantages and disadvantages to the option of selling an institution. The church affiliation is lost with the sale of both Lambuth and Martin Methodist to state institutions, as is the mission to nurture spiritual development in students. However, in the case of Martin Methodist, the campus community is preserved; this was not true for Lambuth. Most importantly, since there was no four-year public institution of higher education in southern Tennessee between Chattanooga and Memphis, Martin Methodist's mission of educating young adults and serving an underserved region will continue as a public institution.

These examples describe the option of selling an institution to the state. But it might be possible for United Methodist institutions to affiliate with other United Methodist or even other private institutions.

In an era of remarkable educational technologies accelerated by the COVID-19 pandemic, institutions might be able to affiliate with one another to create innovative models of higher education. What if one of our larger United Methodist universities and smaller college campuses across a region developed a joint operating agreement? What if some of our smaller colleges allied to become distant campuses of a new, overarching United Methodist institution?

Even as this chapter goes to press, there is consideration of the Claremont School of Theology in southern California selling to or affiliating with Willamette University in Salem, Oregon. This suggests (though Claremont is not an undergraduate-serving institution) that it might be possible to continue the mission of intellectual and spiritual development in a residential, undergraduate setting while sharing costs across distant campuses.

The extent to which the original mission of United Methodist institutions continues under the possibility of a sale to another institution depends on the circumstances. Sale to or a merger with a state institution, as with Lambuth or Martin Methodist, means an end to the mission of spiritual development of students. Yet, the mission of educating students and serving the broader community continues. Sale or alliance with a United Methodist institution would mean continuing the holistic mission of the institution, including spiritual development. Still, without further research, it is unclear whether cost savings would be sufficient to merit such an approach.

Leaving the Church

One other option is for institutions to disaffiliate from the United Methodist Church. United Methodists' commitment to nonsectarian higher education, centering on the guarantee of academic freedom, was once an advantage. However, recent conflict in the United Methodist Church over full inclusion of church members and leaders who identify with LGBTQI+ communities means that United Methodist affiliation for colleges and universities has become a liability. The reality of sectarian constraints on campus life or dogmatic boundaries on academic freedom at United Methodist institutions now seems more likely as limits to true diversity and full inclusion are debated in the church. In addition, as noted above, once there were significant advantages to affiliation with the United Methodist Church, including a pool of potential students and significant financial support. As the church has become smaller and members are older, these advantages have disappeared. Disaffiliation becomes a more attractive possibility as the struggle about full LGBTQI+ participation in the church makes United Methodist affiliation a burden, paralleled by the fading benefit of prospective students and financial support from United Methodist congregations and conferences.

Randolph College, formerly known as Randolph-Macon Women's College, in Lynchburg, Virginia, decided to disaffiliate from the United Methodist Church in June 2019. In late February 2019, after the General Conference voted to pursue the Traditional Plan and continue to exclude members and leaders identifying with LGBTQI+ communities, Randolph issued a statement reiterating the college's commitment to nondiscrimination in admissions and hiring. In the statement, the college also distanced itself from the action by the General Conference, declaring, "This decision to discriminate against and demean others does not have any impact on our commitment to the full human rights of every member of our community." Then, in June 2019, Randolph's Board of Trustees voted to sever all ties with the United Methodist Church, declaring that the General Conference decisions "contravene the fundamental principles of nondiscrimination, diversity, and inclusion to which Randolph College is committed." The statement ended with a reiteration of Randolph College's affirmative commitment to include individuals of various identities.

The legalities of disaffiliation of a United Methodist higher education are complex, and I am not a lawyer or an expert on the United Methodist Book of Discipline. However, paragraph 2501 of the 2016 Book of Discipline states that all institutions are held in trust but may be released from that trust. From public documents available from Randolph College and the Virginia Annual Conference, it is unclear whether the Virginia Annual Conference took action to release Randolph from the deed of trust. Perhaps that legal action is still in process. There are no reports from Randolph in the Conference Journal for the 2020 session of the Virginia Annual Conference suggesting that the separation was complete by then.

However, in the case of Martin Methodist College, the Tennessee Annual Conference, on the advice of the Conference Board of Trustees and Conference Board of Higher Education and Campus Ministry, passed a resolution affirming the plans of the college's board of trustees to join the University of Tennessee system and releasing the college from the deed of trust. This resolution cleared the way for the Martin Methodist board and University of Tennessee governing authorities to complete the merger and made it possible to preserve the campus community nearly intact.

The conflict in the United Methodist Church over the full inclusion of members of LGBTQI+ communities and the inevitable schism of the church can be a liability for United Methodist institutions. It may be, especially given the loss of past advantages to church affiliation, that disaffiliation is more consistent with the educational mission, academic freedom, nonsectarian spiritual development and diverse and inclusive communities institutions seek to nurture. The Book of Discipline provides a way for annual conferences or other authorities to release institutions from the deed of trust. However, the process may need to be tailored to fit the legal situation of individual institutions.

Conclusion

Even before the present conflict in the United Methodist Church, many United Methodist institutions of higher education confronted existential uncertainty. Over the past decade, United Methodist institutions have dealt with increasing costs, decreasing affordability, declining enrollments, fewer diverse students, and falling completion rates, especially for diverse students. These trends are concerning in and of themselves, even if United Methodist institutions were not also dealing with the repercussions of conflict over full inclusion of LGBTQI+ identifying members and leaders in the United Methodist Church. That uncertainty is further complicated by the suspension of decision-making forced on the church by the COVID-19 pandemic.

The decisions of the 2019 Special General Conference stand for now because of the delay of the 2020 General Conference. Both conservative and progressive United Methodist leaders have moved to establish alternative connections and parallel organizations, indicating that neither side anticipates the survival of the United Methodist Church as it is currently constituted. The Protocol of Reconciliation and Grace through Separation, widely expected to serve as the roadmap for schism, speaks to the continuing affiliation of higher education institutions.

Article IV, section 1, subsection b seems to suggest that colleges will remain affiliated with annual or jurisdictional conferences regardless of the institution's decision. It is entirely conceivable that a United Methodist institution of higher education will find itself affiliated with an annual or jurisdictional conference with which it fundamentally disagrees. If the protocol ultimately does guide the actions of the General Conference, then amendments need to be made that will release institutions from their deeds of trust and allow institutional boards of trustees to determine if affiliation should be continued.

In the landscape of American higher education, Methodist higher education is a distinctive model: the importance of educating both the head and the heart, through academic rigor and spiritual development, for service in the world. For those institutions that remain affiliated with Methodist churches in coming years, there will need to be full support from the United Methodist Church and its successors. A pool of potential students and reliable financial support could make a significant difference for many of our institutions. For those institutions that choose to disaffiliate, there needs to be a graceful and straightforward process that allows institutional leaders to make the best choices for their college or university. In this way, institutions of higher education founded on the Wesleyan way that unites "knowledge and vital piety" will continue to thrive.

Chris Donald is the University Chaplain and Director of the Center for Spiritual and Religious Life at Vanderbilt University, and an elder in full connection in the Virginia Annual Conference. He has served large and small local congregations, ministered in healthcare settings, and held several roles in public and private higher education.

Chris holds an MDiv from The Divinity School at Duke University and a doctorate in higher education administration and policy from the Peabody College of Education and Human Development at Vanderbilt University.

CHAPTER EIGHTEEN

The Future is Made of the Same Stuff as the Present

Rebekah Miles

Simone Weil, the mid-20th century Christian mystic and philosopher, wrote of the temptation to make a false God – an idol – of the future. We are tempted, she writes, to think that when the future brings a release from the hard things or the gift of abundant good things, all will be well. We are only able to believe this, she says, "because we lie to ourselves. If we really reflect for a moment, we know it is false." As compelling and lovely as the future may seem, Weil calls us to remember a simple fact: "The future is made of the same stuff as the present."[1]

For all the things dividing us as United Methodists (traditionalists, centrists, and progressives alike), we share a deep longing to move beyond our current impasse. We long for the future when we can distance ourselves from the fights and focus again on our mission and ministries. That is a good and holy thing for which to long.

But if we think the future will solve our problems, we are lying to ourselves. "The future is made of the same stuff as the present." Moving into the future, we will carry the scars of our recent conflicts and the ways that we have been distorted by them. Moreover, many of the troubles that got us into these difficulties will remain within the United Methodist Church, the Global Methodist Church, and any other denominations that might emerge.[2] After all, "the future is made of the same stuff as the present."

---

[1] Simone Weil, "Some Thoughts on the Love of God," *On Science, Necessity, and The Love of God*, Richard Rees, transl., Oxford University Press, 1968.

[2] I am focusing here on the United Methodist Church and the Global Methodist Church. It had appeared that there would be a new progressive denomination, the Liberation Methodist Connexion, but in a statement released on December 18, 2021, "The LMX, Where are We Now," leaders indicated that they didn't have "the structure or resources" at this time. See www.thelmx.org/the-lmx-a-year-in/.

Here are some potential temptations and dangers that I see as we move toward the future:

Shared Temptations and Dangers

Many of us – from across the United Methodist spectrum – have fallen into the bad habit of demonizing the opposition – maximizing their excesses and annoying habits while conveniently overlooking our own. In C.S. Lewis' intriguing *Screwtape Letters,* the older and wiser demon, Screwtape, offers advice to his less experienced nephew demon about leading humans astray. One proven strategy is to steer people into a "settled habit of mutual annoyance." You must "see to it that each of these two fools has a sort of double standard….Hence from every quarrel they can both go away convinced, or very nearly convinced, that they are quite innocent." [3]

This is an ugly habit and harmful to our souls, which is bad enough, but there is another cost. Demonizing our opponents and overlooking our own complicity can distort our corporate vision as we move toward the future. As often happens when fighting becomes bitter, the different sides tend to polarize and become negatively shaped by the conflict. There is a tendency to go too far in the opposite direction and leave important things behind.

Temptations and Dangers for the Global Methodist Church

For the Global Methodist Church, the temptations and dangers may include creating an overly centralized enforcement mechanism with little due process (a reaction to the recent practice in some parts of the United Methodist Church to not enforce the disciplinary provisions regarding LGBTQ marriage and ordination); becoming overly focused on sexuality and sexual practice; giving so much authority to the local congregations that the denomination becomes congregationalist and loses its Methodist connectionalism; and neglecting the great Methodist tradition of social transformation. I'll focus here only on this last point.

---

[3] C.S. Lewis, Letter 3, *The Screwtape Letters* ,Harper Collins, 1996.

One of the great opportunities of the Global Methodist Church will be to offer an evangelical option that combines personal piety, evangelism, and social witness; holding these things together has been a hallmark of Methodism. The flip side of that opportunity is the danger that the Global Methodist Church will, perhaps as a reaction to their long fight within United Methodism, de-emphasize social witness, especially as it goes beyond the transformation of the individual Christian and includes the transformation of the world. There is some reason to be concerned.

The various draft mission statements of the Global Methodist Church (and its originating body, the Wesleyan Covenant Association) are instructive. Since 2008, the United Methodist mission has been to "make disciples of Jesus Christ for the transformation of the world."[4] In all of the available drafts of the *Book of Doctrines and Discipline,* the second half of the mission statement is dropped: "for the transformation of the world." The first available drafts, *The Book of Doctrines and Discipline for a New Methodist Church* (November 2019 to December 2020), changed the mission statement from the current form "to make disciples of Jesus Christ for the transformation of the world" to the simpler and quite different – "to make disciples of Jesus Christ in the world" as well as a slightly amended version – "to make disciples of Jesus Christ in the entire world." The 2021 drafts of the *Transitional Book of Doctrines and Discipline of the Global Methodist Church* offer the mission statement that is now widely used by the Global Methodist Church, this time replacing "to make disciples of Jesus Christ for the transformation of the world" with "to make disciples of Jesus Christ who worship passionately, love extravagantly, and witness boldly."[5]

Once again, "for the transformation of the world" is missing, but perhaps one could interpret "love extravagantly" as including that social transformation. Several points argue against this, however.

---

4   The United Methodist Church, "The Mission," ¶ 120, *The 2016 Book of Discipline of the United Methodist Church,* United Methodist Publishing House, 2016.

5   *Book of Doctrines and Discipline for a New Methodist Church, Version 1.0,* November 8, 2019 https://wesleyancovenant.org/wp-content/uploads/2019/11/Doctrines-and-Discipline-Version-1.pdf; *Book of Doctrines and Discipline for a New Methodist Church, Version 1.1,* December 3, 2020. https://wesleyancovenant. org/wp-content/uploads/2020/12/Doctrines-and-Discipline-Version-1.pdf; Transitional Book of Doctrines and Discipline of the Global Methodist Church, Feb 1, 2021 https://peopleneedjesus.files.wordpress.com/2021/02/82948-englishtransitionalbookofdoctrinesanddiscip line_.pdf; *Transitional Book of Doctrines and Discipline of the Global Methodist Church,* May 11, 2021, https:// peopleneedjesus.files.wordpress.com/2021/05/790c1-englishtransitionalbookofdoctrinesanddiscipline.20210511. pdf; *Transitional Book of Doctrines and Discipline of the Global Methodist Church,* October 10, 2021, https:// globalmethodist.org/wp-content/uploads/2021/10/Transitional-Discipline.20211010-1.pdf.

First, in the early drafts of the Wesleyan Covenant Association mission statements, it is clear there was a decision to drop the language "for the transformation of the world." That was done intentionally and is not a big surprise. Some of the traditionalist United Methodists opposed the addition of that phrase when it was recommended in advance of the 2008 General Conference. Second, the social witness statement in the *Transitional Book of Doctrines and Discipline of the Global Methodist Church* is remarkable for the absence of any emphasis on broader social transformation.[6] Others have remarked on how short the Global Methodist Church social witness statement is. (The United Methodist Social Principles are twelve times longer than the proposed Global Methodist Church "Social Witness" section.)

The most striking thing about the Global Methodist Church social witness statement, however, is not the limit in the number of words but in scope. The Global Methodist Church statement is focused primarily on changing the lives of individuals and naming sin, but it offers very little about changing broader society and social structures. The statements on racism are a good example. *The Transitional Book of Doctrines and Discipline of the Global Methodist Church* includes a denunciation of racism (along with several other isms) in this 45-word statement. "We believe that all persons irrespective of their station or circumstances in life have been made in the image of God and must be treated with dignity, justice, and respect. We denounce as sin racism, sexism, and other expressions that unjustly discriminate against any person." The United Methodist statement, by contrast, in addition to acknowledging the value of all persons and denouncing the sin of racism, also outlines systemic as well personal aspects and calls for broader social change with some specific recommendations. Thinking about human sin and responsibility broadly and socially is a hallmark of Methodism.

Given the evidence, there is reason to be concerned that the Global Methodist Church will neglect the Methodist emphasis on social transformation. Of course, this is not a done deal. We only have a draft of the *Transitional Book of Doctrines and Discipline* to review, and the Global Methodist Church is not yet a denomination. We may find that the Global

---

[6] "Social Witness," ¶¶ 200 and 201, *Transitional Book of Doctrines and Discipline of the Global Methodist Church*, October 10, 2021.

Methodist Church, by the time it becomes a church, is deeply concerned about "the transformation of the world." That is my hope and prayer.

Temptations and Dangers for the United Methodist Church

For the United Methodist Church of the future (post-separation), the temptations and dangers could include neglecting accountability and enforcement (in reaction to the harsh enforcement and penalties of the traditional plan); continuing to try to maintain a large bureaucratic structure it can no longer afford, especially with the double financial hits of COVID-19 and the Global Methodist Church departure; and continuing to struggle to find unity in a very diverse church while not fully embracing its Wesleyan heritage and theology as it casts a vision for a big-tent church. I will focus here on this last point.

The most common Global Methodist Church charge against the current and future United Methodist Church is that it is, and will be, doctrinally weak. What's odd about this claim is that the leaders of the Global Methodist Church, who have often criticized the doctrine of United Methodist Church, have offered in their *Transitional Book of Doctrines and Discipline* a near identical set of primary authoritative documents that make the *very same* key doctrinal claims. There is nothing at all different about the doctrine. The differences are not about doctrine itself but the mechanisms for enforcement.

While the Global Methodist Church leaders are wrong in their criticism of United Methodist doctrine, they are getting at a potential problem. After whatever division awaits us, the Global Methodist Church will be relatively homogenous, but the United Methodist Church will still be a big-tent church with people of very diverse perspectives, cultures, and even theologies. The danger with any "big-tent" group is that it will de-emphasize its core identity and values. This has been perceived as a problem, for example, in the Democratic party. Democrat Alexandria Ocasio-Cortez, complaining about Joe Biden and other centrists to conservative members of her party, opined, "Democrats can be too big of a tent."[7]

---

[7] David Freelander, "Alexandria Ocasio-Cortez Reshaped her Party's Agenda, Resuscitated Bernie Sanders's Campaign, and Hardly has a Friend in Town," *New Yorker Magazine*, January 6, 2020.

George Lakoff, in his best seller, *Don't Think of an Elephant! Know Your Values and Frame the Debate,* argues that a central problem with the Democrats is that they have often failed to explain their positions in relation to a larger frame of meaning and core values. For Lakoff, frames are "mental structures that shape the way we see the world" and often include metaphors or narratives; embedded within these frames of meaning are key shared values. The big-tent Democrats, Lakoff charges, have tended to promote their policies without articulating the larger values and framework behind them.[8]

All this talk of framing and broader narratives, metaphors, and values should sound familiar to Christians because that's what Christian theology provides – a way of seeing the world that comes along with a rich array of stories, images, and values. (It is a way of seeing, I should add, that we believe is true and represents how the world really is.)

One of the potential dangers for United Methodism as it moves into the future, embracing the reality of a big-tent denomination, is that in an attempt to "be all things to all people," it will not fully embrace and emphasize the broader framework and values that support it. In the interim between the special session of General Conference 2019 and the expected General Conference of 2020, United Methodist historian Kevin Watson wrote of his fears for the continuing United Methodist Church. "I suspect that one of the legacies of The United Methodist Church will be its stripping away of specificity and a detailed account of Methodist doctrine and discipline in favor of its attempt to erect a big-tent Methodist Church."[9]

I hope and trust that The United Methodist Church will prove its critics wrong and continue to move forward with a strong emphasis on the theological claims at the heart of the *Book of Discipline of The United Methodist Church* and the Methodist movement itself. Certainly the statements of doctrine will remain the same. And I have seen reason for hope in recent months, especially within the Council of Bishops.

Bishops in the United Methodist Church are our teachers and "are

---

[8] George Lakoff, *Don't Think of an Elephant! Know Your Values and Frame the Debate*, Chelsea Green Publishing, 2014.

[9] Kevin Watson, "Methodism Is in the Details: Moving from Breadth Back to Depth," Aug 13, 2019, https:// kevinmwatson.com/2019/08/13/methodism-is-in-the-details-moving-from-breadth-back-to-depth/.

authorized to guard the faith, order, liturgy, doctrine, and discipline of the Church" (¶ 403). In their November 2021 statement, "A Narrative for the Continuing United Methodist Church," they are ably fulfilling those responsibilities.[10] While the Bishops emphasize the "big-tent" nature of the continuing United Methodist Church, they frame unity and diversity entirely in relation to Christian language and values, drawing on Scripture and our communion liturgy; affirming our doctrinal standards; and emphasizing key Methodist claims while completely avoiding the language of a big tent. "We are a holy communion of different races, ethnicities, cultures, and perspectives united by the Holy Spirit, driven by the mission of Christ, and bearing the good news of an unmerited grace that changes lives and transforms communities." We move forward as a church, "confident in what God has done in Christ Jesus for all humankind;" "committed to personal and social salvation/ transformation;" and "courageous in dismantling the powers of racism, tribalism, and colonialism." The bishops have set forward a compelling theological narrative, giving an account of what has long undergirded our big-tent church.[11] Of course, it is still (and always) an open question whether United Methodists are willing to be led by their bishops.

A few days before the overwhelming approval of "A Narrative for the Continuing United Methodist Church," Bishop Cynthia Fierro Harvey gave her address as the president of the Council of Bishops at the opening session of their meeting.[12] She highlighted many themes of the Narrative and offered a further theological framing. Bishop Harvey noted that big-tent United Methodism was in the midst of a storm. "It's time to face the reality that our Big Tent is having a little trouble holding up to the winds of change. And amid this windy season, we must work harder than ever before to honor and respect one another, making space for each other, reinforcing our big tent, digging deeper, creating an even stronger rootedness in the presence of Christ."

---

[10] The Council of Bishops of the United Methodist Church, "Narrative for the Continuing United Methodist Church, November 4, 2021, www.unitedmethodistbishops.org/files/websites/www/a+narrative+for+the+continuing+united+methodist+church.…._.pdf.

[11] United Methodist Communications recently released a new campaign and hashtag – #BeUMC that is in keeping with the themes of the bishop's "Narrative for the Continuing United Methodist Church." See www.umc.org/en/what-we-believe/umc-topics/our-people/beumc.

[12] Bishop Cynthia Harvey, Presidential Address, Fall Meeting of the United Methodist Council of Bishops, November 2, 2021. Video available at https://www.facebook.com/watch/live/?ref=watch_permalink&v=40542126.

Like the bishops in their shared statement, Harvey made it clear that this rootedness is in Christ and that the reinforcement of the big tent must come from our theological vision. To support this vision of a diverse United Methodism united in love, Harvey drew on 1 John 4:19, "We love him, because he first loved us." John Wesley prized 1 John, describing the book as "the deepest part of the Holy Scripture" and both a "compendium of all the Holy Scriptures" and of "genuine Christianity."[13] And within 1 John, this verse was the most important. It was, he proclaimed, "the sum of all religion, the genuine model of Christianity. None can say more: why should anyone say less."[14] 1 John 4:19 – and the whole of 1 John – emphasizes the centrality of God's love for all and the deep and necessary connection between God's love for us and our love for God and others.

Harvey quotes at length from an essay by John Wesley, "A Plain Account of Genuine Christianity," that paints a vision of a true Christian, and it is all about love.[15] Wesley wrote this essay in a dispute with Conyers Middleton over doctrine and the authority of the church fathers. Wesley canceled a trip to Amsterdam and spent twenty days writing an extremely long and remarkably tiresome essay, but in the final pages, he offers a moving reflection on the ideal Christian that became a classic among Methodists. In *John Wesley*, Albert Outler writes of this essay:

> *After some sixty pages of academic disputation, Wesley switches his argument from the analysis of patristic texts over to a quite different line. The one point he really cared to make is that actual Christian faith and life, not only in apostolic and patristic, but also still in modern times, reflects the supernatural power of God and the miraculous presence of the Holy Spirit (182).*

For Wesley, being a Christian is, above all, about love. Human love, along with every other good thing in the world, is made possible by God's prior love through the power of the Holy Spirit. God's loving presence undergirds it all. This is no minor theme for Wesley but is at the heart of

---

[13] John Wesley, *Journals and Diaries, Volumes 21 and 22*, W. Reginald Ward and Richard P. Heitzenrater, eds. in *The Bicentennial Works of John Wesley*, Abingdon Press, 1992 and 1993. See 17 July 1765 and 9 November 1772, in *Journal 22*: 13 and 352 as well as 30 August 1763, in *Journal 21*.

[14] John Wesley, 1 John 4:19, *Notes on the New Testament*, The Methodist Book Room, 1805.

[15] John Wesley, "A Plain Account of Genuine Christianity," *John Wesley*, Albert Outler, ed., Oxford University Press, 1980.

his understanding of God, the world, and the Christian life.

In the section quoted by Harvey, Wesley seeks to offer the "plain, naked portraiture of a Christian," and this Christian portrait centers around generous, abundant love.

> *Above all, remembering that God is love, he is conformed to the same likeness. He is full of love to his neighbour: of universal love, not confined to one sect or party, not restrained to those who agree with him in opinions, or in outward modes of worship, or to those who are allied to him by blood or recommended by nearness of place. Neither does he love those only that love him, or that are endeared to him by intimacy of acquaintance. But his love resembles that of him whose mercy is over all his works. It soars above all these scanty bounds, embracing neighbours and strangers, friends and enemies.*

For the ideal Christian, this love drives everything else. Love produces the fruits of the spirit; it drives a commitment to fulfill duties to others; it is the source of right action and guides Christians to a "uniform practice of justice and mercy." Are there points of disagreement between Christians? The "opinions" that divide are "but of small concern and do not enter into the essence of his character. Cover them with a veil of love and look at the substance."

How is this extraordinary love possible in human life? Only by the presence of the Holy Spirit and the human response in faith, by the "power wrought by the Almighty in an immortal spirit inhabiting a house of clay." This confidence and optimism in the power of God's love working through us by the Holy Spirit and the subsequent transformation in human lives and in the world are at the heart of Methodist identity. That hope is more than enough to support the biggest of tents.

Weil is no doubt right that the future is made of the same stuff as the present, and that is both our caution and our hope. That present, when rightly understood, includes not only our disasters and failures but also the best of our shared heritage and, especially, the presence of God. As we move forward – the Global Methodist Church, the United Methodist Church, and any other denominations that emerge – we will bring all of it, the present and immediate past, our long-shared heritage, and above all, the empowering presence of the Holy Spirit. That is reason for hope.

Rebekah Miles is Susanna Wesley Professor of Practical Theology and Ethics at Perkins School of Theology, Southern Methodist University.

Dr. Miles is author of several books, including *The Bonds of Freedom: Feminist Theology and Christian Realism* (Oxford University Press, 2001); *Georgia Harkness: The Remaking of a Liberal Theologian, Collected Essays* (Westminster John Knox, 2012); *The Pastor as Moral Guide* (Fortress Press, 1999); *The Routledge Companion to Christian Ethics*, with Steve Long (Routledge Press, 2023); and *When the One You Love is Gone* (Abingdon Press 2012); in addition to other edited and co-authored volumes and numerous articles, especially around Methodist studies, realist ethics, and practical theology.

CHAPTER NINETEEN
The Quiet Middle of Methodism

Randall Partin

Quiet
(from the musical, "Matilda")

Have you ever wondered (well I have),
about how when I say, say "red"
(for example), there's no way of knowing if red,
means the same thing in your head,
as red means in my head when someone says, "red" . . .

And when everyone shouts (they seem to like shouting),
the noise in my head is incredibly loud.
And I just wish they'd stop . . .

And the heat and the shouting.
And my heart is pounding.
And my eyes are burning
And suddenly everything, everything is. . . quiet

like silence, but not really silent.
Just that still sort of quiet.
Like the sound of a page being turned in a book.
Or a pause in a walk in the woods.

Quiet.

Like silence (but not really silent).
Just that nice kind of quiet.
Like the sound when you lie upside down in your bed.
Just the sound of your heart in your head.

183

The pandemic-caused delays of our United Methodist General Conference have generated a sort of uneasy quiet (not unlike the eye of a storm), a quiet that has given many of us an opportunity, hopefully, to consider "…the sound of our heart in our head."

To start with, I empathize with the frustration and disappointment of my friends and colleagues across the ideological and theological spectrum: those for whom delay of legislative action means further injustice and exclusion; those for whom delay of legislative action means lack of clarity about doctrinal standards; as well as those for whom delay means, more than anything else, continued, prolonged turbulence and discord.

I also notice, however, that these past months have been an opportunity for deeper discernment, listening, and (indeed) wonder. In my preaching, I have found that some of my most-uttered phrases are either "what if" or "I wonder …" Much of what follows will be that sort of wondering, a wondering borne of a certain quietness that has allowed many of us to be still, to consider, to imagine. I would never claim or consider that these wonderings are original, or even remotely mine alone, but I would hope that these wonderings might find a certain resonance among others and that we might find that these ideas in my head might be the same as or similar to the ideas in your head as well.

I no longer wonder whether the United Methodist Church will separate or change significantly through some form of dissolution or restructuring. It will. I confess that over the years, my thoughts, emotions, and preferences have been all over the place, from my first General Conference in 1996 – where the politics of the global denomination spooked me from answering a call to ministry – to the profound and deeply moving signs of unity amid strife at the 2004 General Conference, to 2016 and 2019 when it felt like the whole denomination was going to come unglued. I have hoped for unity. I have longed for division. I have lamented our frustrating inability to work across (or through) our differences, and I have prayed that we might separate ourselves as peaceably as possible.

In these past few months, certainly since 2019, but even more so in the relative quiet of the past two years, I have become less and less troubled with the prospect of division. I have become resigned (but hopefully resigned, if that makes sense) that sometime soon, we will no longer be together in the same way. For those of us contemplating a "post-separation" United Methodist Church, I seriously hope that we are wondering what sort of structural embodiment of Methodism will serve us best going forward – a structural embodiment that is fundamentally more agile, fluid, and "flatter" than our current institutional arrangements which have bound us so, so tightly and, frankly, made some of our disagreements even more intractable. What might a more simplified governance structure (that maintains our core values of representation and inclusion) look like? What of our current structure and polity is absolutely essential to moving forward? What should be modified? What should we leave behind? I wonder.

That said, I have rarely (if ever) wondered if a purely legislative/institutional solution to our current impasse will suffice. It won't. While legislation and action of General Conference might be a necessary condition for bringing forth whatever our shared future might be, legislation alone will not pave the way for that future. At best, legislation can create the metaphoric hardware for us to reconfigure ourselves; but the critical software – especially the relational and pastoral aspects – will be more important for us to figure out and should require some serious attention and wonder as well.

Separation or restructuring will be much more complicated (and messy) than many of us have imagined. Indeed, I suspect some of us are learning just that in this quiet season. This will be true regardless of how much energy and attention has already been poured into many of the legislative proposals. Clarity about the extra-legislative and relational aspects of our shared life together on the other side is something worth investing some serious energy and wonder in, wherever we currently might land in our state of division.

For example, as a practical matter, what possibilities for sharing clergy and recognizing orders across our next structures might exist? In some of our annual conferences, clergy or churches will quickly (or not so quickly) be "orphaned," finding themselves part of a different structure than their preferred ideological or theological "home." How, for the sake of missional effectiveness, could we work together now to create the means for appointing or sending clergy across our anticipated divides?

Similarly, where will we share missions, programs, structures on the other side of a divide? How will we share? What will we share? In my own annual conference, I hope that our much-loved camp and conference center (Sacramento), not to mention the stellar Lydia Patterson Institute (an entity of the South Central Jurisdiction), will continue to be supported and sustained by all of us on the other side of what lies ahead. Committing to such mutual sharing and support now would be a bold step into an uncertain future and create opportunities for collaboration and cooperation going forward, no matter what.

Further, what are the pastoral care needs for all of our churches and leaders (clergy and lay) that will have to navigate extremely difficult conversations and decisions, particularly as we come out of a global pandemic where so many of our leaders are already flat-out exhausted emotionally and spiritually? How will we pay attention to (and tend to) the grief of ruptured relationships between clergy colleagues and friends, within congregations, Sunday school classes, etc.? Paying attention to these relational, pastoral dynamics – at least as much as we have paid attention to the legislative/structural questions – will be vital to how we all navigate this future.

In a similar vein, I think it is worth acknowledging (and figuring out) how much we continue to have in common across our divides. I hope we might cultivate further opportunities for conversation beyond separation and restructure – and quickly. A colleague who attended the opening gathering of the Wesleyan Covenant Association came away with the sense that even as we have moved towards separation and distinction across our differences, most of us agree on 90-plus-percent of what we share in common.

While we have spent so much time these past few years talking past or about each other, I hope that post-separation, we might take time to reach out and talk with each other, to describe and define the contours of what our shared Wesleyan identity might be for the benefit of all of us on the other side of our divisions. What would it look like to collaborate across our divides on a joint, shared restatement of something like our Theological Task? What would it look like to work towards some of the contours of full communion partnership, especially on the heels of any division or separation? Recognizing how much we continue to share in common, jointly articulating those commonalities might help us all with the relational aspect of our life together beyond division.

Some have drawn the analogy of an impending "divorce" in United Methodism. I'm not so sure that such an analogy serves us all that well. To be sure, there are legal, technical, and institutional analogs (division of property and assets, for example), but there is so much more to our current unhappy state than these technical, legal, or institutional matters – much, much more. Even families experiencing divorce have to navigate the tender nature of relationships post-separation and recognize that "family" stretches beyond the brokenness. Similarly, we should tremble with the knowledge that we are rending the body. We should lament that our disunity diminishes our hoped-for glory as the bride of Christ. Whatever lies on the other side of our current season, we will still be family together, we will still be (all of us) part of the Body of Christ in the world, and we will still be part of the same church that awaits the coming of the bridegroom, that longs for the same heavenly banquet – no matter our differences.

What should be clear is that much of my wonderings assume or expect a desire for further conversation and collaboration even across – especially across whatever divisions lie ahead of us. It reflects my current circumstances of serving a local church that has always understood itself and aspires to be a "big tent" congregation. It also reflects being part of an annual conference (the New Mexico Annual Conference) that has, sometimes to a fault, strived to emphasize and maintain collegiality across our differences.

I suspect, however, that a vast majority of all our people, our churches, even our annual conferences also fall into the broad middle of Methodism that has kept largely quiet during much of the shouting. That is not to say that our differences are not significant enough to preclude division. Instead, I simply wonder if a reasoned conversation about some of the extra-legislative, noninstitutional, or "softer" dynamics of division – or, indeed, how we continue to work together across and after division – is in order.

I wonder, also, if you might have some of the same thoughts in your head as well. I wonder.

Randall W. Partin is the Senior Pastor of St. John's United Methodist Church in Albuquerque, New Mexico. Prior to being appointed to St. John's in July of 2021, Randall served as the Provost and Director of Congregational Vitality for the New Mexico Annual Conference (2015-2021).

Through sheer happenstance, Randall attended and had the privilege of serving on staff for every General Conference from 1996 to 2016. In 2018, he was elected the first clergy delegate to General Conference from the New Mexico Annual Conference.

CHAPTER TWENTY

Can an Annual Conference Disaffiliate From the Denomination Under Church Law?

William B. Lawrence

A few months before the called session of the United Methodist General Conference in February 2019, the Judicial Council reviewed legislative proposals for changes in church law and for amendments to the church Constitution. All were driven by the divisions in the denomination over human sexuality. In Decision 1366, the Judicial Council ruled on the constitutionality of the proposed legislation, which three groups had drafted and submitted as petitions.

Among the legislative proposals on which the Judicial Council ruled was a petition from "Traditional Plan" advocates that would have made it lawful for an annual conference to leave (or secede from) the denomination. Specifically, Petition 90041 proposed that a new ¶ 2801 be added to the *Discipline*. According to the proposal, ¶ 2801.9a would begin as follows:

> *Any annual conference may become a self-governing church or join an existing one when that annual conference votes by simple majority to seek this status under the terms of this paragraph.*[1]

This was one of two petitions[2] that would have permitted an annual

---

[1] Thomas A. Lambrecht, Traditional Plan 90041, *Advance Daily Christian Advocate.*

[2] Petition 90041 was submitted by the Commission on a Way Forward through Thomas A. Lambrecht. It was "Not Supported" by the Standing Committee on Central Conference Matters, to which it was assigned. The announced vote on the motion of Non Support was 28 (for the motion), 4 (against the motion), and 5 (not voting). The second, Petition 90078, was submitted by Maxie Dunnam. It was "Not Supported" by the Standing Committee on Central Conference Matters, to which it was assigned. The announced vote on the motion of Non Support was 32 (for the motion), 0 (against the motion), and 4 (not voting). Petition 90078 was rejected by the General Conference plenary on February 26, 2019, at 6:25 PM. The vote was 314-482. Both 90041 and 90078 proposed a new paragraph 2801 in the Discipline. The Addendum to *The Book of Discipline* 2016, published after the 2019 General Conference, does not contain that proposed paragraph.

conference to leave. It would have provided the procedures, including the proportion of favorable votes needed, for an annual conference to approve disaffiliation. But the General Conference did not adopt it.

Judicial Council Decision 1366 ruled that Petition 90041 was constitutional. But it never became a law. After the 2019 General Conference ended, Decision 1378 reviewed its actions but ignored Petition 90041 because it was merely a legislative proposal that had been defeated.

Most judicial bodies, like the United States Supreme Court, can only rule on matters that involve the constitutionality or merits of laws enacted by legislatures. But The United Methodist Church allows the Judicial Council to rule on proposed legislation as well as on actual laws. The jurisdiction and powers[3] of the Judicial Council, under church law, include its "jurisdiction to determine the constitutionality of any proposed legislation when such declaratory decision is requested by the General Conference or the Council of Bishops."[4]

Yet, any decision on proposed legislation is preliminary and tentative. Despite a Judicial Council ruling in advance that finds a petition constitutional, the General Conference might still amend the item before approving it, or it could reject the petition entirely. Since an amended and adopted petition may differ constitutionally from the proposal that had endured Judicial Council scrutiny, it could receive further review. And if General Conference rejects the petition entirely, the church is left with a Judicial Council decision that is irrelevant because there is no law to which it applies. The ruling is a fact, but it has no effect, for it does not affect any actual law.

That is the dilemma with Petition 90041. The General Conference did not enact it as law. That means Decision 1366, to quote the Judicial Council, is "an historical precedent." But it is not a permanent principle. As Decision 1366 says,

> an historical precedent may have symbolic and moral force for practical considerations but can hardly serve as legal authority to determine the validity of future decisions. If past actions of the General Conference are precedent-setting in the sense that they supply the constitutional justification for similar actions in the future, it would enable the General Conference to unilaterally

---

[3] *The Book of Discipline of The United Methodist Church 2016* ¶ 2609.

[4] *The Book of Discipline of The United Methodist Church 2016* ¶ 2609.2.

modify the Constitution without going through the amendment process of ¶ 59 in violation of the separation of powers. Thus, any past, current, and future decision of the legislative branch of the Church is not a decisive factor in constitutional adjudication.[5]

The Absence of Church Law on Annual Conference Disaffiliation

Though no church law exists regarding an action by an annual conference to disaffiliate from The United Methodist Church, advocates of the concept have insisted on its validity based on Decision 1366. Some propose new legislation for it. Others say no legislation is needed.

1. An Authorization in Proposed New Legislation

The authors of the "protocol" took the first approach. In the draft legislation that they prepared for submission to General Conference as a petition, they proposed a new paragraph in the *Discipline* with specific procedures for annual conferences in the United States and in the Central Conferences to leave the denomination. In a proposed ¶ 2556.4a, the legislation drafted by "protocol" authors specifies:

An annual conference may, by a vote of 57 percent of the lay and clergy members present and voting at a regular or called session, choose to separate from The United Methodist Church to form or join a New Methodist Denomination. The annual conference shall consider this decision upon motion from the floor that is supported by one-fifth of its lay and clergy members present and voting or may do so through its normal processes. The annual conference may also call a special session for this purpose upon motion from the floor or through its normal processes. If the annual conference does not vote to separate by July 1, 2021, it shall by default remain part of The United Methodist Church.[6]

It is important to note that this proposed legislation was drafted with the expectation that the General Conference would meet as scheduled in May 2020. Since the Commission on the General Conference has rescheduled the gathering to a time after the deadline specified in this proposed legislation, the draft from the "protocol" would have to be amended by deleting or revising its date of expiration.

---

[5] Judicial Council Decision 1366, page 43. The amending process is established in Division Five of the Constitution.

[6] The draft legislation was submitted to the General Conference by three annual conferences. The authors of the "protocol" and its legislation were an *ad hoc* group who had no authority to send late petitions to the General Conference. But a provision in ¶ 507.6 of the 2016 *Discipline* permits an annual conference to do so.

It is also important to note that the authors of the "protocol" proposed procedures for its implementation. The threshold for final approval of a motion to disaffiliate would be 57% of the annual conference lay and clergy members casting votes. The persons who would be eligible to vote would be "the clergy and lay members" of the annual conference. And taking the vote on whether to approve annual conference disaffiliation from the denomination would be mandatory if any member offers a "motion from the floor that is supported by one-fifth of its lay and clergy members present and voting." So, 20% of the lay and clergy members of the annual conference could impose an order on an annual conference to act in a regular or called session to disaffiliate. Then 57% of all the clergy and laity voting would be enough for it to secede.

The authors of the "protocol" cite Judicial Council Decision 1366 as justification for this proposed legislation. They assume that, because Petition 90041 was found to be constitutional in advance of the February 2019 General Conference, their legislation is constitutionally valid even though it proposes things that differ from details in Petition 90041. They would set a threshold of 57% as the required percentage of clergy and lay votes to support disaffiliation, for example. It is proposed legislation, of course, rather than a proposed constitutional amendment. Therefore, it would need just a simple majority of votes from General Conference delegates to approve it.

2. An Authorization Based on Legislative Silence

Others who are enthusiastic about the concept that an annual conference can disaffiliate from the denomination insist that no such legislation is needed. In a few annual conferences, at least, clergy and lay members are ready to propose and support their conference action to leave The United Methodist Church. A few bishops seem prepared to rule that motions are in order for an annual conference to leave, and they are ready to exercise authority as presiding officers to say what the threshold for approval of such a motion would be, absent any stipulation in law.

This is an argument from silence. It interprets the Constitution and the Discipline of the church as documents that permit actions unless they specifically prohibit actions. It assumes that if the Constitution and laws are silent, the silence provides sufficient authority to act.

This view expands on Decision 1366. In ruling that Petition 90041 was constitutional, the Judicial Council noted the different types of authority that the Constitution establishes for all the conferences in the polity of The United Methodist Church. In brief, the General Conference has "full legislative power for all matters distinctively connectional,"[7] the jurisdictional and central conferences set the boundaries of annual conferences in their regions and elect bishops who are assigned to the areas in their jurisdictions,[8] and the "annual conference is the basic body in the church" with the authority to determine who are the clergy members and the ordained ministers in the church.[9] Decision 1366 chose to see a level of significance in an annual conference as "the basic body in the Church" that exceeded the significance of jurisdictional or central conference authority to define annual conference boundaries.

To some advocates of an annual conference's right to disaffiliate, this is enough, given that the *Discipline* is silent on the point and the process. Its silence, they say, empowers an annual conference to withdraw its clergy members from The United Methodist Church and to remove the lay members of local churches in it. According to this view, actions are permitted unless some law explicitly prohibits them, and any act is allowed unless it is explicitly banned. These United Methodists argue that an annual conference can vote to disaffiliate because the *Discipline* says nothing about it and because the Constitution does not prohibit it.

However, legislative silence is not a hallmark of Methodist discipline. After Methodism in America separated – with his permission – from John Wesley's control in 1784, the power to legislate was exercised by the General Conference. Initially, that was all the preachers. Later, it became a delegated assembly. Now The United Methodist Church has a globally representative legislature with votes equally shared by clergy and lay delegates elected in annual conferences.

For nearly two-and-a-half centuries, the General Conference has codified expressly in church laws what is permitted and prohibited.

---

[7] The Constitution, Division Two, Section II, Article IV, published in *The Book of Discipline of The United Methodist Church 2016* as ¶ 16.

[8] The Constitution, Division Two, Section IV, Article V, published in *The Book of Discipline of The United Methodist Church 2016* as ¶ 27.4, and also Division Two, Section V, Article IV, published in *The Book of Discipline of The United Methodist Church 2016* as ¶ 31.4.

[9] The Constitution, Division Two, Section II, Article IV, published in *The Book of Discipline of The United Methodist Church 2016* as ¶ 33.

Methodists have enacted laws against enslaving people, using tobacco, consuming alcohol, and engaging in sexual abuse, among other things. Such laws, like ¶ 2553 which permits a local church to disaffiliate from The United Methodist Church, have defined the procedures to be followed for their implementation and enforcement.

The Role of Law in the Wesleyan Theological Tradition

Methodists write laws for theological reasons. Wesley, like Calvin, saw that one purpose of law is to provide guidance for the well-ordered and disciplined practice of Christian life.[10]

The church laws in the Discipline are like the Ten Commandments and the teachings of Jesus, in form. Torah put the law both in positive terms to require constructive actions ("Honor your father and your mother") and in negative terms to prohibit destructive actions ("Do not kill").[11] Jesus defined discipleship both positively ("...love your enemies") and negatively ("don't blow your trumpet as the hypocrites do").[12] The church puts "unauthorized conduct" by pastors positively (they "shall first obtain the written consent of the district superintendent...") and negatively ("Ceremonies that celebrate homosexual unions shall not be conducted...").[13]

In Wesley's theology, believers cooperate and collaborate with the gifts of God's grace to engage in a process of salvation. The General Rules[14] are do no harm, do good, and attend to the ordinances of God. They are spiritual practices for a believer seeking salvation. They construct a positive law that blends with grace. They define the disciplined way of life that embodies Jesus' command to "Go and do likewise" after he told the parable of the Good Samaritan.[15]

The *Discipline* expresses these positive laws in two different forms. Some are mandates that use the word "shall," meaning "must." Others use the word "may" to indicate that an act is permissible but not mandatory. In the "General Provisions" regarding pastors'

---

[10] Wesley believed that "the truth of the gospel" is "within a hair's breadth" of Calvinism. (Minutes of the Bristol Conference, August 2, 1745, *The Works of John Wesley*, Abingdon, 2011.

[11] Exodus 20:12-13 and Deuteronomy 5:16-17 *(Common English Bible)*.

[12] Matthew 5:44 and 6:2 *(Common English Bible)*.

[13] *The Book of Discipline of The United Methodist Church 2016* ¶ 341.

[14] *The Book of Discipline of The United Methodist Church 2016* ¶ 104.

[15] Luke 10:37 *(Common English Bible)*.

appointments, for instance, Section X of Chapter Two in the *Discipline* says "Appointments to Various Ministries" differ based on ordination. The law distinguishes elders in full connection, all of whom "***shall*** be continued under appointment," from others who "***may*** be appointed..."[16] Distinctions between "shall" and "may" occur throughout the Discipline, impacting local and connectional matters.

Moreover, the Constitution establishes the governance systems of The United Methodist Church in positive and negative forms. Most clauses in the Constitution are constructive and positive: jurisdictional and central conferences "shall have" the power and duty to set boundaries of annual conferences; annual conferences "shall have" authority to decide "all matters relating to the character and conference relations" for clergy members; "bishops shall appoint, after consultation with the district superintendents, ministers to the charges." But there are negative clauses, too. They are especially notable in the "Restrictive Rules."

Introduced in 1808, the "Restrictive Rules" are the oldest constitutional clauses in Methodism. They establish in unequivocal terms what the General Conference "shall not" do.[17]

For any church in the Wesleyan tradition, including The United Methodist Church, to be an instrument of grace requires engaging in the practices of faith and honoring its disciplines.[18] We trust grace, we develop methods for teaching grace, and we shape disciplined practices for doing the work of grace. We hold one another accountable for honoring our disciplines, as we have from the earliest class meetings to the present annual conferences. Once, class leaders asked each member, "How is it with your soul?" Now, in current clergy sessions of annual conferences, the question is, "Are all the clergy blameless in their life and administration?"

As a church that believes and conveys grace in the disciplines of life, Methodists expect one another to write and to honor the rules. They include the Constitution and the legislation of United Methodism. Where the *Discipline* is silent, it is a sign that we have not yet crafted some

---

[16] *The Book of Discipline of The United Methodist Church 2016* ¶ 337. The emphasis is added.

[17] Other Methodist denominations besides The United Methodist Church retain them.

[18] At John Wesley's first "conference" in 1744, the agenda consisted of three questions: What to teach? How to teach? What to do?

spiritual discipline or defined some faithful practice for an action.

The Constitution Speaks

But is it silent on the authority of an annual conference to leave the denomination? The church speaks to the issue in at least three specifically established powers in the Constitution. Two of them are positive, constructive statements. One is negative and prohibitive.

- It vests in the jurisdictional and central conferences the authority to define the boundaries of annual conferences.[19]

- It defines the authority to vote on clergy membership and ordination as being limited to select lay and clergy members of an annual conference.[20]

- It prohibits the General Conference from taking any action to deprive lay and clergy members of their right to trial before removing them.[21]

It is essential to examine these clauses with care. They bear directly on claims of annual conference authority to take a vote and make its own decision to exit from the denomination. An advocate of proposed legislation (like the petition linked to the "protocol") or an advocate of the annual conference right to secede based on a claim of legislative silence must address what the Constitution establishes.

FIRST, church law in *The Book of Discipline* defers to the Constitution of the church explicitly with reference to the "powers and duties" of jurisdictional conferences.[22] Within the Constitution, jurisdictional conferences in the United States and central conferences in other countries of the world are established with the authority to set the boundaries of the annual conferences within their geographical regions. If an annual conference assumed for itself the authority to leave the denomination, the boundaries of the annual conferences adjacent to it would be altered because they would be erased. It would be

---

[19] The Constitution, Division Two, Section IV, Article V, and Division Two, Section V, Article IV, published in *The Book of Discipline of The United Methodist Church 2016* as ¶¶ 27.4 and 31.4.

[20] The Constitution, Division Two, Section VI, Article II, published in *The Book of Discipline of The United Methodist Church 2016* as ¶ 33.

[21] The Constitution, Division Two, Section III, Article IV, published in *The Book of Discipline of The United Methodist Church 2016* as ¶ 20.

[22] *The Book of Discipline of The United Methodist Church 2016* ¶ 525.

unconstitutional for an annual conference to exercise power that belongs to the jurisdictional or central conference. It would impact adjoining annual conferences by depriving them of the voice and the vote that they are constitutionally given in a jurisdictional or central conference regarding boundaries.

If one of the five annual conferences within the state of Texas were to claim that it could vote to disaffiliate from The United Methodist Church, the other annual conferences in the state (as well as, perhaps, in one or more neighboring states) would be deprived of boundaries that had been defined by the South Central Jurisdictional Conference, which is the only entity that has the constitutional authority to define annual conference boundaries. The Constitution has constructed the jurisdictional and central conferences and has given them that authority. Annual conferences cannot usurp that authority.

SECOND, the Constitution of The United Methodist Church establishes that "all matters" regarding United Methodist clergy and their ordination are reserved to the annual conferences. In that same article, it establishes those within the annual conference who are eligible to vote on "all matters" concerning clergy membership and ordination. The Constitution excludes, with a very few specifically identified exceptions, "lay members."

If an annual conference were to act on a motion of disaffiliation from the denomination and were to permit "lay members" to vote on the motion, it would unconstitutionally bestow on those "lay members" an authority that the Constitution withholds from them. To put it another way, if an annual conference were to adopt a motion to disaffiliate from The United Methodist Church by allowing unauthorized voters to cast ballots, it would exercise power it does not have to authorize lay voting rights for removing clergy members from the United Methodist ministry.

That constitutional violation would exist whether the annual conference created its own rules for determining eligibility to vote or borrowed proposed legislative language (perhaps from the "protocol") that is contrary to Division Two, Section VI, Article II (published as ¶ 33) in the Constitution. What is established in the Constitution cannot be overruled by an action taken in an annual conference, regardless of the enthusiasm that votes by laity and clergy may show for it.

THIRD, there is nothing that can be stated or implied by the General Conference within its legislative work that deprives clergy or lay members in The United Methodist Church of their rights to a trial. But an annual conference vote on a motion to disaffiliate from the denomination would do exactly that. It would remove lay members of local churches in the annual conference from The United Methodist Church and place them in whatever religious affiliation the motion stipulated. And it would remove clergy members of the annual conference from any membership in the Christian church because clergy have their church membership in annual conferences.

It would take these actions while it unconstitutionally deprived the clergy and laity of their right to trials. Such a deprivation of rights could open the door to more complications than an internal church feud about definitions of membership or preferences about sexuality. It could open the door to possible litigation in civil courts. Any clergy member who is an ordained elder could cite the harm that was inflicted by being deprived of an annual appointment at no less than minimum compensation without a trial. Indeed, class-action lawsuits could embroil components of the church beyond the annual conference that took the vote to disaffiliate.

A Necessary Step

For an annual conference to vote to leave the church, neither a presumption about some silence in the Constitution and *Discipline* nor a proposed piece of church legislation can grant sufficient power to do so. For an annual conference to disaffiliate from the denomination, the Constitution will have to be amended. Then some enabling legislation might define valid procedures for doing it.

Under current church law, a local church may depart from The United Methodist Church. If it meets the criteria and follows the process for disaffiliation in ¶ 2553, a congregation may leave the denomination. They are at liberty to leave by taking steps in their annual conferences that church law allows. They can depart one local church at a time.

Under the current church Constitution and law, anyone who is a clergy or lay member of The United Methodist Church may leave. Any individual lay member may exit from The United Methodist Church by withdrawing from membership in one's local church. Any clergy member may exit by surrendering one's ministerial credentials and withdrawing from membership in the annual conference, and hence from the denomination, at any time. Clergy can seek to transfer to other denominations that will convert their United Methodist credentials to the new sect.

However, if an annual conference seeks arbitrarily on its own initiative to depart from the denomination, or if the General Conference tries to enact legislation that would permit annual conferences to disaffiliate, such actions will violate the current Constitution in at least three ways. Therefore, constitutional amendments will be needed before legislative actions at the General Conference or self-declared actions in annual conferences can occur legitimately.

The church would have to address the constitutional authority that presently exists over annual conference boundaries, address the constitutional authority for voting on clergy membership and ordination, and address constitutional restrictions on removing clergy and lay members without their rights to trial. Such amendments will require a two-thirds vote by the General Conference delegates and approval from two-thirds of the aggregated votes from annual conferences in the entire connection.

These things can be done. But they are not merely matters of constitutional or legislative activities that impose rules on spirituality. In the Wesleyan theological approach, they are actual expressions of spirituality. Through the disciplines of faith, Methodists embrace God's grace and are saved by it.

William B. Lawrence is an ordained Elder in The United Methodist Church and a clergy member of the North Texas Annual Conference in the retired relationship. He was a pastor in New York, Pennsylvania, and Washington DC, in addition to serving as a district superintendent. About half of his active ministry was in appointments at academic institutions, including fourteenyears as dean of Perkins School of Theology at Southern Methodist University.

He is now professor emeritus of American Church History at Perkins and a research fellow at the Center for Studies in the Wesleyan Tradition at Duke Divinity School. He served a term on the Judicial Council and for four years was its president. He and his wife, Naomi, live in Chapel Hill, North Carolina.

CHAPTER TWENTY-ONE
Freedom Through Prayer

Sue Nilson Kibbey

Jesus said, "Let the little children come to me,
and do not hinder them,
for the kingdom of heaven belongs to such as these."

Matthew 19:14 (NASB)

It began in 1707.

In England at the time, John Wesley was just three years old.

In Central Europe, efforts for economic, political, and spiritual recovery continued underway following the ravages of the Thirty Years War. The war had been an extended, savage, bloody religious battle now remembered as one of the most violent conflicts in the church's history, with more than eight million deaths from combat, disease, and famine. In the end, the battle's actual motivation had not been primarily about faith and doctrine but instead about the politics and resultant power struggle regarding which group would ultimately govern Europe.

The population of Silesia, a small European nation sandwiched amid Saxony, Prussia, Poland, Bohemia, Moravia, Austria, and Hungary, was left ragged, impoverished, and starving. Church parishes had been destroyed. Countless young Protestant children, orphaned and oppressed by the aftereffects of the war, roamed the countryside and mountains grappling for food, means of work, and – as history reveals – spiritual focus.

It was in 1707 that an extraordinary, unplanned spiritual phenomenon began. Silesia's children spontaneously began to gather together on their own to read Scripture, sing hymns, pray, and recite Protestant catechisms and liturgy they had memorized in earlier times when families had been intact, and parish worship had been more available. The children, ages four to fourteen years old, came together twice or more daily from everywhere, out in the open. Lying prostrate on the rocky ground, they prayed to God for breakthroughs that would bring peace and religious freedom. According to eyewitnesses, the ragtag children prayed fervently and plainly for a deliverance miracle, and adults within sight would stop and watch the children with awe.

To be clear, the children's prayer gatherings were not wildly emotional or loud. The children were described as calm and devoted. Their gatherings were not organizationally structured. Rather, the children simply centered their prayers together on asking God, repeatedly and expectantly, for spiritual awakening, divine rescue, and for themselves to become God's living messengers.

The Silesian children's prayer movement, or "Kinderbeten" (children's prayer) as it came to be called, continued organically for eight months until early 1708. Unbeknown to them, during that same time, an unexpected and favorable wrinkle in the political navigation for possession occurred on behalf of the Protestant Silesian churches. A negotiated legal provision behind the governmental scenes resulted in the unexpected arrival of Swedish military troops into Silesia to bring urgently needed social and religious stabilization to the area.

Upon witnessing the soldiers' arrival, the children understood this to be a miraculous answer from God to their prayers for deliverance. The Kinderbeten-led revival mushroomed, sweeping in only five days across the entirety of Silesia with children pouring from the mountains and filling the streets, praying everywhere. Religious authorities encouraged the children to find churches in which to take their activities. Thus the prayer-fueled revival further spread across all ages as it moved into and through Silesian Protestant congregations. Countless new believers were spiritually drawn to receive faith in Christ and became engaged in ongoing, collective, vibrant discipleship. The initial spiritual awakening that began in Silesia with the children's prayer ranged much wider over the next three decades, manifesting fresh, exciting church renewal into other parts of Central Europe. Notably, renewal was often instigated first by similar outbreaks of children's prayer for revival.

Jesus said, "Let the little children come to me,
and do not hinder them,
for the kingdom of heaven belongs to such as these."

One of those places was a new Christian community in neighboring Moravia named Herrnhut. Led in its early years by Count Nikolaus Ludwig von Zinzendorf, the small village struggled at first to find unity in faith and spiritual direction. A lay leader at Herrnhut, Christian David, was familiar with the historical impact of the Silesian children's prayer movement and that country's resultant spiritual awakening. He began to beseech God, asking for just such a prayer awakening among the children of Herrnhut. He believed their surrendered prayers would initiate the breaking down of barriers and usher in full and genuine spiritual revival, rippling out to excite everyone in the new community of Herrnhut to prayer.

God answered Christian David's prayer in the summer of 1727 through the spiritual awakening of a Herrnhut resident, 11-year-old Susanne Kuhnel. Susanne and three other young Herrnhut girls individually experienced a breakthrough conversion to Christ the very same evening. These conversions initiated a wave of awakening prayer, uniting all the children of Herrnhut later that night, soon spreading to engage those of every age in prayer for a personal, community, and global spiritual awakening beyond what they could ask, think, or imagine.

Over the ensuing one hundred years, the small community of Herrnhut, convinced of the transforming power of prayer, organized and perpetuated an unbroken prayer chain every hour around the clock. During the next decades, out of Herrnhut emanated an estimated 226 lay missionaries who felt called to embark to every part of the known world at that time, setting up Bible studies and prayer initiatives that indeed fruitfully took the message of Christ beyond the limits of their human imaginations. Out of the prayer movement at Herrnhut was birthed the first lay Protestant missionary crusade in church history.

Jesus said, "Let the little children come to me,
and do not hinder them,
for the kingdom of heaven belongs to such as these."

John Wesley was one of the untold numbers who encountered Christ in a whole new way via the Herrnhut lay missionary efforts. Grown now, he had become a discouraged Anglican priest at the crossroads of faith and vocational next steps. Wesley gained new assurance of life in Christ and the life-changing power of the Holy Spirit through a Moravian lay-led prayer and Bible study in England. His later on-site visit in 1738 to Herrnhut to observe and meet personally with Christian David influenced the eventual shaping of the new Methodist movement Wesley promulgated – especially Wesley's emphasis on the centrality of prayer for all followers of Christ, including children.

The incredible story of the Silesian children's prayer movement in an environment of fracture, loss, weariness, change, pain, and transition is only one example (among countless others throughout Christian history) of what truly provides foundational fuel for the spiritual movement we know as the church of Jesus. The deeply surrendered, corporate prayer of God's people – setting aside personal preferences, judgments, and plans to ask instead for the Almighty's preferred new possibilities to break through – is the heavenward request the Holy Spirit awaits.

Ongoing, foundational, collective prayer like this sets the stage for God's church, and every congregation, to look up and out with expectancy for God's response and with surrendered openness to receive communal discernment of courageous next steps forward onto the open road of an unknown and miracle-filled new future.

What's next for our church today amid fracture, weariness, denominational questions, and shifts? Through the priority of moving unadorned, spiritually yielding prayer to the center of our congregations and of our individual lives, we are freed to become like the praying Silesian children whom God used to usher in deliverance, renewal, and direction during change and transition. Like them, the fruit of our completely surrendered prayers can transform us into living messengers of Christ's love together.

Jesus said, "Let the little children come to me,
and do not hinder them,
for the kingdom of heaven belongs to such as these."

The historical segment of this chapter's content was originally researched and prepared as part of my doctoral thesis work at United Theological Seminary in Dayton, Ohio. I am especially grateful to Dr. J. Steven O'Malley, author of *The Origin of the Wesleyan Theological Vision for Christian Globalization and the Pursuit of Pentecost in Early Pietist Revivalism* (Lexington, KY: Emeth Press, 2020), which contains new primary source material that contributes illuminating details to the account of the Kinderbeten, Herrnhut, and John Wesley's connection.

Rev. Sue Nilson Kibbey serves as Director of the Bishop Bruce Ough Innovation Center at United Theological Seminary in Dayton, Ohio.

Sue is a nationally-recognized trainer, consultant and author of multiple books and resources. Her greatest passion is igniting congregational momentum of what she terms a "Breakthrough Prayer Initiative," which has been the foundational heartbeat of the Missional Church Consultation Initiative (MCCI).

She is the author of *Open Road: The Adventure of a Breakthrough Prayer Initiative* and *Flood Gates: Holy Momentum for a Fearless Church.*

CHAPTER TWENTY-TWO
Yet We Have Hope

Walter Cross

It was a very pleasant Saturday in autumn in the middle of the 1950s, and I was just a wee little tike. My assignment in that early morning was to assist my mother in preparing food for the church's annual homecoming meal.

My father had recently deposited a 10-pound bag of sweet potatoes in the kitchen, along with a bushel of green beans. I was assigned to help my mother with the prep work, and I scraped the sweet potatoes, which she later cut up and put in a big pot of water to boil. I really wasn't that much help. My mother could have done the job all by herself, but she was helping to entertain me on a Saturday. She knew how to take a green bean, snap it, and pull that long string off of it. I could snap a green bean, but my string would always tear off.

The end result of the basket that went to the church the next day was a layer of aluminum foil on the bottom, covered by a clean kitchen towel. My mother transformed those ten pounds of potatoes into four delicious sweet potato pies. I saw every one of them when they went in the oven and when they came out. She used real butter – not margarine like we usually got. They smelled like vanilla, nutmeg, ginger, and all the delicious ingredients.

Next to the pies were two chickens. Two fryers cut up, plus six extra wings. My mother would fry the chicken to perfection in an old black skillet till those caramelized brown pieces would form on the bottom. She would flip the chicken over so easily, with no flash, no pop. That was layer one: the warm layer.

Next, there was a cool layer. On Sunday morning, she put a layer of ice, then twenty-four deviled eggs. Of course, we couldn't take deviled eggs to church, so we called them angel eggs. On top of the angel eggs was a tray of carrots, sweet pickles, and the relish tray. The relish tray had celery, creamed cheese, and little bitty olives. Next to that tray was a group of toothpicks with Vienna sausages, stuffed olives, and a cube of cheese. They were all lined up like little soldiers. That was the cool layer. She covered that with aluminum foil and another insulating towel.

I got to look at all that food, and it all went to the preacher's table right after church that Sunday afternoon. I didn't get to eat with the group at the church. I sat with the organist in the sanctuary while he practiced, and the people downstairs were eating food. I was only five years old, and I would eat my meal at home.

My hope was – yes, there is hope – that there would be something left over from all that chicken and all those pies and all those green beans – that there would be something left for me. I lived in hope. But as the day passed by that Sunday, hope began to wane. The preachers were hungry. They asked for seconds. They asked for thirds. Then, they asked for some to take home. When I went to take the baskets to the car, there was nothing left in the baskets but those towels and some crumpled aluminum foil. I was sad.

I sat in the back seat of the car, thinking, "I'm going to dine on bologna crackers tonight," which would have been okay if I hadn't seen all the fixings that my mother had prepared for the meal. But I had seen all of that food:

I saw all that chicken.

I saw all those sweet potato pies.

I saw the green beans.

I saw all the fixings my mother had made and those homemade brown-and-serve rolls.

And there I sat with an empty basket. My hope was crushed. I sat silently as we went home.

"Walter, Junior. Are you alright?"

"Yes, ma'am."

"Boy, what's wrong with you?"

"I'm okay, Dad."

I went into the house and sat at the table, anticipating my bologna crackers. My mother looked at me. She almost smiled, but she kept a stern look. She opened the oven. In the back of the oven was pie number five, three chicken wings, and a corner piece of cornbread. Oh, I was so happy.

She looked at me again and said, "You thought you got left out."

Always remember, there is something for you at home. There is always something for you at home. Patience helps develop hope.

When I turn in my Bible to Romans, the writer is dealing with a situation plaguing the Christians. There's an influx of culture there. The Greek culture and the Roman culture. There's this new movement called "The Way," there's a myriad of doctrines, and sometimes it left the new Christians confused. They were plagued with different opportunities of doctrine. The Old Testament scholars wanted them to adhere strictly to the Law. It turns out that the Law was neither a friend to them nor a friend to us.

So, Paul steps in and says, "I need to explain something to you all. You all are in a hopeless situation because you've found out you can't keep the law. You're being terrorized by individuals in the religious community who are forcing the law upon you, and they know that you can't keep it because they can't keep it. Your situation appears to be hopeless."

Paul comes to the rescue in Romans, chapter 8. That chapter is the rescue chapter for hopeless Christians. Paul gives a list of items that are difficult to deal with. Then, in verse 24, Paul says, "There is yet hope. Hope is not something that you can see."

There are two types of hope in the Bible, and there are two types of hope in our lives today. I may hope to win the lottery one day – I don't know how because I don't play the lottery. Winning the lottery is a hope that is defined by chance.

I hope I get a good grade. I hope Publishers Clearing House stops by my home and knocks on the door. I hope I get that new car.

That's not what Paul is talking about.

In the New Testament, the word "hope" means a certainty. It means it is already done. It means God has handled the situation for us.

My hope is built on nothing less
than Jesus Christ and righteousness.

My salvation is done by the finished work on Calvary. I don't hope to be saved. I am. I don't hope to go to Heaven. I'm on my way. Not because of my goodness. It's because – as the writer says – there is nothing remaining that can separate me from the love of God. Not peril, not destruction, not even the idea that we stand on this moment at the brink of World War III. That won't separate me. Not because of the scourge of this dreaded disease that has been sweeping our world for the last three years.

That's not going to separate me from the love of God.

- Racism is not going to separate me.
- Hateful speech is not going to separate me.
- Who's president is not going to separate me.
- Who's not the president is not going to separate me.
- What's happening in my family – what's happening in my heart – will not separate me from the Love of God.

It's a done deal.

Yes, I'm going to have some difficulties and pain. I'm going to have trials. I can tell you; this is not an easy road from Earth to Heaven. But, I yet have hope.

Some may say, "All the churches are going to close, and pastors will be out of their jobs." But I'm not going to say, "I hope not," in response. I will say, "Whatever happens, I have hope."

Jesus told us to do three things that instill hope in us. Those three things are to:

- Love God with all my heart, mind, and soul.
- Love my neighbor as myself. I like me, and I'm going to treat you like I treat me. I'm not going to misuse you.
- Make disciples.

I don't have time to lay down and have a pity party. I can't talk about "woe is me." I yet have hope. Am I upbeat every day? No. Am I blind to reality? No. I understand everything that's going on. I stand beside an open casket. I look inside at one of my loved ones. My heart is broken. But as I leave the cemetery, as sad as I might be, I yet have hope because Jesus is life.

I have hope for eternal life. But I've learned that we also have hope in this present age. We don't have to wait to cash in at the Pearly Gates. We can enjoy the presence of Christ now. There will be difficult days, but there's never going to be a day without Jesus. Because Jesus is always there, I yet have hope.

Let me ask you something. As you read this book's final chapter, after reading all of these wonderful scholars, you may find yourself asking, "What is Walter Cross talking about?"

As you read these few words, you may be interested, but you may feel hopeless. You may be looking and searching, but you feel hopeless. You may be wondering, "Who cares for me? Who loves me?"

It's no accident that you've picked up this wonderful book. It is the providential Will of God that you read these words.

Yet, there is hope.

There's hope for you.

There's hope now, then, and when you need the Lord on your side.

That's what I want to share with you about the certainty, the reality, and the security of hope.

God bless you.

Pastor Walter Henry Cross,
otherwise known as "Old Rugged Cross"

Rev. Walter H. Cross Jr. is pastor of Lonsdale United Methodist Church and Martin Chapel United Methodist Church, both in the community of Lonsdale in Knoxville, Tennessee.

Pastor Cross answered the call to preach in 1992. He attended Emory University, Candler School of Theology in Atlanta, Georgia, completing Pastoral Course of Study. He serves as a mentor for candidates pursuing ministry in the United Methodist Church.

Pastor Cross is the husband of The Reverend Dr.Angela Hardy Cross and the father of Walter Elijah Cross and wife Eboni Cross and Granddad of Walter Elijah Cross II.

Epilogue

Kevin Slimp

I'm honored to count several writers of this book as friends. Walter Cross and I met twenty years ago when I served on the Holston Conference staff. We were reacquainted just a year ago when his wife, Angela, now a district superintendent in Holston Conference, contacted me about a book Walter had recently published. One thing led to another, and Walter and I were soon reacquainted.

I was surprised to learn that Walter has lost much of his eyesight in recent years. Shortly after our twenty-year reunion, I called Walter, asking him to participate in writing a chapter for this book. He contacted me a few days later and asked if I would meet with him and record the words as he spoke them, entering the words into the computer afterward. So, we met and recorded Walter's chapter. Afterward, I told a friend at church that as I listened to Walter, I felt as if I were hearing one of the greatest sermons I'd ever heard, given just for me – an audience of one.

I typed Walter's words exactly as he spoke them. There were no notes, no prompting, and no breaks. I can still hear his first sentence, "It was a very pleasant Saturday in autumn in the middle of the 1950s, and I was just a wee little tike."

A few days ago, I had the privilege of having lunch with a friend who is a pastor of one of the largest United Methodist churches. I asked how his congregation is dealing with the potential split in the denomination. Without hesitation, he looked straight at me and said, "We're not going to deal with it. We've got too much work to do for the Kingdom. That's where we need to put all our energy, not worrying about what other churches are going to do."

When I tell non-Methodists that I publish books for United Methodists, more times than not, I notice a slightly pained look across their faces. Usually, they will respond with something like, "I hear your church is splitting," or something along those lines, followed by something like, "How will that affect your company?"

For the past few years, my answer has been much like my friend's response at lunch. I answer honestly: "I've got too much work to do. I don't have time to worry about that."

Sue Nilson Kibbey wrote about the importance of moving prayer to the center of our congregations and individual lives. Randall Partin reminds us that we will still be family, whatever happens at the next General Conference. Rebekah Miles writes that for the ideal Christian, love drives everything. Ryan Spurrier thinks we must reclaim our Christian character. Tori Butler reminds us that we are called to enter each other's pain.

Kim Goddard insists that we must fulfill our mission. Douglas Meeks writes that we already know the end of the story. Rebekah Simon-Peter thinks we have an opportunity to find new ways to be the church. Stephen Handy believes the future is filled with more people, not less; more diversity, not less; more young people, not less. Melanie Dobson reminds us of the roots of Methodism and how we can reclaim those roots. Wil Cantrell says the church is in the life-transformation business.

Rodney Smothers believes it is time to recommit to leadership development. Bishop Kenneth Carder believes we need to move beyond slogans and marketing campaigns to shift the margins of the denomination's ministry.

Kay Kotan reminds us not to place limitations on what God can do with God's church. Kristin Joyner writes that we need to be arguing for more love in the world, not less love. Laceye Warner reminds us that with faithfulness to God's call comes joy.

Thank heavens for great thinkers like Thomas Frank, William Lawrence, and Christopher Donald, helping us understand the realities our church faces in very practical matters about which most of us never think.

Bishop Richard Looney began this book by reminding us that God is good, even "within the maddening maze of things."

Walter Cross believes it is the providential Will of God that you are reading this book. After being so inspired by his words – and the words of so many others in these chapters – I'm not going to argue.

Our Newest Title from Market Square Books

REBEKAH SIMON-PETER

EMBRACING THE NEXT NORMAL

forging
a new path

moving the church forward
in a post-pandemic world

marketsquarebooks.com

Other Titles from
Market Square Books

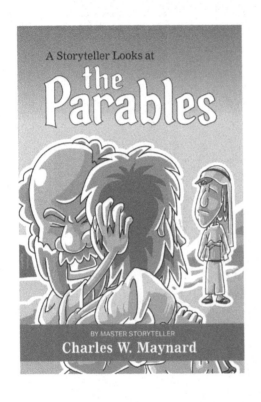

marketsquarebooks.com

Other Titles from Market Square Books

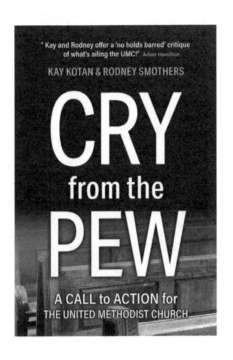

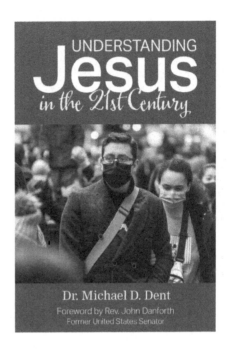

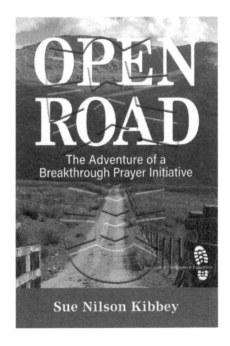

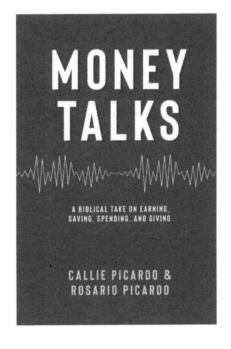

Other Titles from
Market Square Books

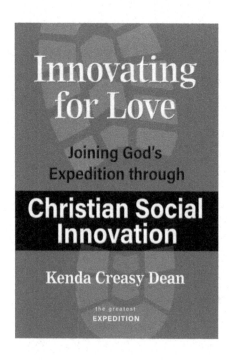

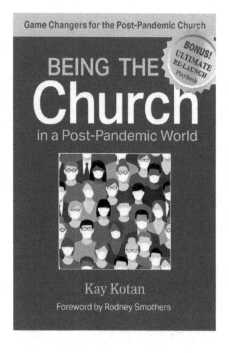